the grandparents' book

book

Making the most of a very special relationship

MIRIAM STOPPARD

DK

LONDON, NEW YORK, MELBOURNE, MUNICH, DELHI

For Eden, Violet, Zac, Brodie, Olivia, Esmé,
Catherine and Hebe, and Maggie and Evie

Editor Jinny Johnson
Art Editor Kathryn Gammon
Project Art Editor Peggy Sadler
DTP Designer Sonia Charbonnier
Senior Jacket Creative Nicola Powling
Styling and design assistance Vicky Read
Production Hema Gohil
Managing Art Editor Marianne Ma'
Art Director Peter Luff
Publishing Director Corinne Robert
Indexer Elizabeth Wiggans
Proofreader Jill Williams

First published in 2006 by
Dorling Kindersley Limited
80 Strand, London WC2R 0RL
A Penguin Company

Paperback edition 2009

A CIP catalogue record for this book is available from the British Library.

ISBN 978-1-4053-5274-1

Cover reproduction by MDP
Printed in China by Hung Hing

Discover more at
www.dk.com

Contents

Foreword

This is a very personal book.

At the time of writing, I'm granny to eight children with two more on the way and this book is a reflection of my love for them. It is intended to be the opposite of didactic. It does, of course, spring from my experience of bringing up my own four sons, but it's much more to do with what my children and grandchildren have taught me.

I've realized that although I've brought up my own family I'm no more than a beginner where my grandchildren are concerned. A grandparent who concedes this won't go far wrong. But it isn't always easy. And from time to time we all have to practise those well-honed skills of biding one's time, keeping one's own counsel and having selective amnesia.

I was ambushed by my emotional reactions to becoming a grandmother. Never had it occurred to me that I would, through my grandchildren, rediscover, revisit, relive the love I felt for my own children when they were babies. And, even more surprisingly, I've seen my children realize anew, as they watch me loving their children, how much I love them. Only grandchildren can complete this loving virtuous circle between parents and children.

Then there's another unexpected bonus of grandparenthood: I've discovered my children to be stunning parents – loving, diligent, thoughtful, caring parents, better than I was in almost every respect.

I have never been so conscious of, and grateful for, the rhythm of life.

1 The joy of grandparenting

Most grandparents would agree that there are few experiences as wonderful as being with, loving, teaching – and learning from – their grandchildren. This joy lies in store for many of us as we grow older.

Becoming a grandparent is worth waiting for. Grandparents are, or can be, the bedrock on which the rest of the family stands, adding stability and encompassing strong and lasting relationships across the generations. They're a kind of human cement which holds the family together, whether nuclear or extended; a family in which a child can grow up secure and loved, where she feels important and listened to. In helping children relate to people of all ages and to be unafraid among friends and relatives who are older, grandparents help prepare them for life outside the nurturing environment of home and family.

Grandparents are the enablers of their grandchildren, encouraging them to develop their personalities and achieve their goals

Grandparents are the enablers of their grandchildren, encouraging them to develop their personalities and achieve their goals. By virtue of their age, grandparents can generally be more patient, philosophical, long-suffering and sympathetic than parents. Handling children with ease is a knack acquired through long practice, and grandchildren love it. The best grandparents have, over the years, honed their skills of interpreting warning signs. They are able to anticipate problems and head them off – and more often than not pacify by distraction and persuade with patience.

"Granny will help"

The fact that grandparents are less stressed means that they have the time to give explanations and the patience to suggest alternatives and help calm a frustrated child who is facing a difficult task. If Granny's mantra is "Granny will help" and she does, the time will soon arrive when your grandchild invites you into her world with, "Granny, help me". And if Grandpa indulges his hobby of gardening or taking the car to pieces with "Grandpa will show you", Grandpa will soon be assailed with "Grandpa, show me". So quite quickly your grandchildren come to see you as their coach, their manager, their cheerleader and their number one fan, and there's no role you'd rather have: you have a place in their hearts no one else can fill.

Your reactions to becoming a grandparent

Nobody warns you about the emotional assault of becoming a grandparent. Oh, you're aware of the truisms. You're more relaxed, patient, long-suffering than you ever were with your own children – yes. You take crises, be they difficulties with breastfeeding, a child who won't sleep or temper tantrums in your stride – yes. And, yes, you can hand your grandchildren back to their parents at the end of the visit. You're not accountable. But those pleasures don't begin to describe what for me has been the greatest thrill of all. What nobody tells you is that through your grandchildren you revisit emotions you thought were lost forever, gone with your fertile years, gone and impossible to regain. You thought.

But through your grandchildren you recapture the love you felt for your own children when they were babies. And maybe I'm getting emotionally incontinent here, but I suspect, rather ashamedly, that my love for my grandchildren may exceed what I felt for my children.

Recapturing the love you felt for them isn't really the whole story. It isn't so much recapturing as reliving, in technicolour. Through all those years of my children growing up, and my love for them growing up in parallel, I never dreamed I'd have the good fortune to be, emotionally speaking, a young mum again, suffused with that consuming, full-throttle mother love.

But BINGO! With the first grandchild it hits you in the face, in the heart and in the head, and I would have to say it's very close to that other state of grace – being in love.

We can all remember being so much in love that like a pigeon you home in on wherever your beloved happens to be on the planet. You cross oceans, scale mountains, travel thousands of miles so that you can meet, even fleetingly. No journey is too difficult. And would I girdle the earth again for my latest love? You bet your sweet life I would. O'er hill, o'er dale, thorough bush, thorough briar. Eleven hours on a plane across eight time zones to Los Angeles just to be in the same space as Esmé, my latest granddaughter, is no price at all to pay. I have no option.

So is there a purpose?

Surely such an all-consuming passion must serve a greater purpose than my own self-indulgence? Assuredly it does. The reason that women live beyond the menopause – the end of their fertile, and as far as our selfish genes are concerned, useful, lives – is in quite large

I became aware of my son...noticing with what ease I seemed to hold **his newborn daughter**

measure to succour our grandchildren. So that while our children are spending genetically useful time having more children, we're designed to live long enough to keep an eye on the grandchildren, without being distracted by either the desire for or the pursuit of fecundity.

This circularity of input and output at either end of our lives is satisfyingly symmetrical and lends unexpected fulfilment and comfort to our later years. It literally is the rhythm of life. And it's rhythmic for more of your family than just you. I gradually became aware of my son, Esmé's dad, noticing, mostly with surprise, with what ease I seemed to hold his newborn daughter; how I could quieten her with a rocking motion honed by years of nursing four sons and six grandchildren; how I instinctively knew when she wanted to lie flat and could recognize the language of her crying. I could almost read his thought bubble. He was getting an unexpected photo of me from a new angle. Then he saw me love his daughter as I must have loved him. Another photo, retrospective this time. And the bubble again.

For my part, I see my dear son as supportive, caring husband and loving, hands-on 24/7 dad. This is so moving. I discover my son as the father he was always destined to be, and he discovers me as the mother I was to him. Another virtuous circle starts spinning. And neither of us wants out. Who could have expected such a pay-off to life? Thank you, Esmé – and grandchildren everywhere.

Biology is on your side

As the menopause happens so early in life compared to other signs of ageing, many scientists (though by no means all) have put forward the suggestion that the menopause might be useful in an evolutionary sense. Childbirth becomes more and more risky as a woman gets older. She is less fit and strong to fend for her babies, so, the theory goes, a middle-aged woman might do better to forgo the risks of childbirth and enhance her genetic legacy by focusing her energies on her children and grandchildren.

One way to test this hypothesis is to look at other mammals. There are several that show this matriarchal usefulness, the best known being elephants, where the benefits conferred on the herd are substantial and have been measured. Elephant society is essentially matriarchal, organized around a stable family unit of cows and their calves. The herd comprises mothers, daughters and sisters – they didn't get together by accident or choice – and males are ejected when they reach adolescence. The group is lead by a large, old female who usually keeps her position until her death, when she's succeeded by her eldest daughter. And while an elephant may bear calves into old age – 60 or more years – the female leaders of the herd live well beyond that – 75 to 80 years.

In other mammals, such as elephants, matriarchal leaders confer substantial benefits *on the herd*

The matriarch This kinship group has evolved for very good reasons. The older elephant matriarch is the protector and defender of her herd because she is more skilled than the younger female elephants at sorting out friend from foe and knowing where to find food and water. The general wellbeing she confers on the herd is seen in groups with the oldest, and presumably the wisest, matriarchs at the helm – the fertile females in these groups produce more young. In elephants, at least, it's easy to see why intelligence was selected for – the matriarch's ability to spot risky situations makes life easier for her companions.

Whales, too, gather in matriarchal schools. Males often move to other groups when they're sexually mature, but females remain with their maternal group for life and, like elephants, females may spend a third of their lives "post menopause". These groups of females communally look after and defend their young, with the oldest matriarchs acting as the libraries of experience and wisdom. Among whales that are hunted by whalers, and the largest (and most knowledgeable) are consistently taken, there are the lowest birth rates. Could these groups have lost their social knowledge and so be less successful?

Female groups Old females comprise a significant part of a whale school, and probably contribute towards its maintenance and the survival of younger individuals. Some females have a post-reproductive lifespan of 20 to 30 years, and we know that these old females go on producing milk for the calves in their group. This enhances school stability and increases reproductive success for female kin.

There are two more animal species that are often seen by scientists as models for human evolution: the olive baboon and the African lion. Both live in groups that revolve around relationships between female relatives. The lion pride centres on a core of female relatives who hunt together, defend their joint territory and raise cubs communally to the point of suckling each other's young. Lion grannies babysit and join their daughters in defending territory. In baboon groups, daughters rank just below their mothers. Grannies often groom their grandchildren and help their daughters maintain their social status by defending them against other females.

Why do some women live so long? But why, even though our average life expectancy was hardly more than menopausal age 100 years ago, have some woman always lived on well beyond the end of their fertile life? Studies are rare and difficult, but a tribe in the Kalahari Desert and another in the forests of Paraguay habitually see 30 to 40 women out of a 100 living around 20 years after the menopause.

These examples of female longevity may be explained by what we see among animals raised in captivity, protected from food and water shortage, extremes of weather and temperature, predators and disease. These animals live much longer than in nature. It may be that when our ancestors gathered into groups, built shelters, hunted together for the good of the community, devised tools and defended territory, females gradually lived longer to become the repositories of wisdom and social knowledge, as well as the carers of their grandchildren, who would carry on their matrilineal legacy.

Evolution is on our side

Maybe it was because I watched my own mother being such a superb grandmother that I became convinced that women lived into old age simply to fulfil this very necessary role and that evolution was the driving force. My instinct, later my conviction, was that we are programmed to live beyond the menopause in order to help our children with their children. Not every sociologist or anthropologist agreed with me, citing the average life expectancy of under 50 less than 100 years ago – far too short a time for evolution to have raised our life expectancy to the 80-plus we enjoy today.

It turns out that a proportion of women have always survived past the menopause. A beautiful study, undertaken by Finnish, UK and Canadian scientists and published in the journal *Nature* in 2004, went a long way to explaining the benefits to younger generations of this female longevity.

My instinct, later my conviction, was that we are **programmed** *to live beyond the menopause in order* **to** **help** *our children with their children*

Childcare, of their grandchildren, seems to be the reason. Drawing on records from the 18th and 19th centuries of communities in Finland and Canada, the scientists found proof that a woman could gain two extra grandchildren for every decade she lived beyond the age of 50. Darwinists would say that these grandmothers conferred greater "fitness" on their children. Evolution, therefore, would favour the survival of women beyond the menopause if it resulted in extra grandchildren. And this is indeed the case in different communities, irrespective of their wealth, class or standard of living.

There's a reason for grandmothers To my mind that in itself would be a great enough justification for grandmothers, but there's more. The research revealed not only that people whose mothers were alive had more babies, but also that a greater number of these grandchildren survived to adulthood. Furthermore, the mothers gave birth to their first child at a younger age than women whose mothers were dead, and the births were closer together. So grandmothers contribute to reproductive output, so to speak. Interestingly, women who lived more than 20 kilometres from their mothers had fewer children, suggesting childcare and advice were important factors.

In the study, the average lifespan of the Finnish grandmothers was 68 and the Canadians 74. I find it incredible that these ages coincided with the time when their children stopped having babies. At that point, from the point of view of evolution, a grandmother loses her "fitness" and so she dies. This grandmother hopes and prays that her family goes on having babies for some years yet.

In one respect grandparents are ***national treasures*** *because we may be the only enduring link with the disappearing extended family*

Grandparents and society

In one respect grandparents are national treasures, because we may be the only enduring link with the disappearing extended family. In our society, and in every other industrial and technologically advanced society, we're living out the end of a revolution that is one of the most profound the human race has ever undergone. It's the overthrow of kinship as the basic principle that binds us together, and it entails the demise of the extended family.

If you or I had lived some 10,000 years ago – a blink of an eye in the three to four million-year history of our species – we'd have been members of a small band of hunter-gatherers, all of whom would have been relatives by blood or by "marriage". This form of social organization persisted through millions of years of evolution because it dealt with the major problem posed by the long period when the human child is dependent on adults and by the relative weakness of the lone adult in a state of nature.

Dependence on parents alone wouldn't have guaranteed a child's survival, since a pregnant or nursing mother isn't mobile, and a father who must hunt cannot at the same time provide protection. The solution to this problem (and one that occurs in nature in a myriad forms) is for the nuclear family of father, mother and child(ren) to be embedded in a group where childcare can be shared, where hunting and gathering can be cooperative and where, if necessary, defence can be jointly organized. Equally obvious is that the natural group to look to for cooperation and support is the family – the extended family.

The all-purpose extended family An extended family exists where more than one generation of parents and children live together, where a child is born into a unit that includes not just parents and siblings but possibly grandparents, aunts, uncles and cousins, depending on circumstances. Traditionally, a family was also the primary working unit; it produced its own food, cared for its old people and educated its own children in its skills and customs. Virtually every function that for us is now performed by school, hospital, social services or the legal system was to be found within the extended family and the network of linked families that made up the wider social group.

The extended family still exists in many parts of the world, but its last vestiges in Britain disappeared with the Industrial Revolution, when family-based cottage industries such as spinning and weaving were rounded up into more profitable factories. Then family ties had to give way to industry's insistence on a mobile workforce, and people had to go where the work was.

Promoting the survival and rearing of our future generations We are only one of many social animals who live in groups based on the family – though, in the case of our modern industrial societies, it is now "was" rather than "is". The kinship systems differ, but the logic is always the same: to provide a stable base in a given territory, where the group can have access to food supply, security and shelter. All social animals, including whales and elephants, have in common a family-based network that promotes the survival and successful rearing of offspring.

What have we lost along with the extended family? One of the features of the extended family, wherever it is found, is the shared care of children. Babies are born into a group and, from birth, they are surrounded by voices and activity and are never short of a pair of arms to hold them. All adults in the group share in the responsibilities

One of the features of the extended family, wherever it is found, is the **shared care** *of children*

of child-rearing and this means that children are constantly made aware of shared values, of accepted codes of behaviour and of being part of a web of kinship that extends far beyond the limits that our nuclear family generally recognizes. Unless you belong to royalty or have made a hobby of constructing your family tree, it's a fair bet that you don't know all the names of your eight great-grandparents, and that your second cousins have dropped off the edge of your known universe – your second cousins being the grandchildren of your grandparents' siblings.

The passing of the extended family from our society means that we're no longer conscious of being at the centre of an extended network of relations with whom we have bonds of varying strengths and with whom we share two-way rights and obligations. The tensions, the generational conflicts, the sibling rivalries, the jealousies, the testing of authority and the emotional wear and tear that are the by-products of human relations could be diffused, and more easily defused, within the layers of a far-reaching family system. In the absence of an extended family, the same conflicts and emotions have somehow to be accommodated within the much closer confines of the nuclear family, and so it isn't surprising that increasingly often it bursts at the seams.

The role of grandparents in the family Grandparents by definition belong to the older generation and in the past had an important role as repositories of history, experience, wisdom, skills, customs and traditions. Where the accumulated knowledge of a society or community is passed on by older to younger generations through example and oral tradition, considerable respect automatically accrues to the elders.

These days, because of the dizzying speed of change resulting from the electronic information revolution, most of us grandparents have our work cut out just to escape being regarded by our grandchildren as cultural dinosaurs from another planet. What we can transmit to them isn't even a tiny fraction of the accumulated knowledge of our society. However, grandparents, along with any other relatives who are willing to play their parts, can at least represent the kind of continuity that gives a child the certainty of having a place in the world, of being bonded to a supportive group. Of course we have to remember that we don't actually belong to our grandchildren's nuclear family – only they and their parents do – and, unthinkable as that might seem to the members of an extended family, we have to be invited in and earn our place.

Why family is so important

We have the genes of social animals. That means that we have instincts (yes, instincts) for living in groups and cooperating with others for survival and satisfaction. Initially the group has to be a kin group, a group related through ties of blood, plus "in-laws", if only because it's difficult to imagine how we'd put together any other sort to ensure the survival and successful rearing of children. It could be argued that the

Grandparents can represent the kind of **continuity** *that gives a child the certainty of having* a *place in the world*

welfare state can currently provide the necessary minimum, but our instincts don't bind us to benefit books, they bind us to people.

Shared genes A widely accepted theory of why we're prepared to act altruistically towards our children and other relations isn't to do with "love", but with the fact that they share our genes and we want to propagate our genes. Every child has 50 per cent of each of her parents' genes, and we share 50 per cent of our genes with our own parents and with our siblings, 25 per cent with our nephews and nieces, and so on. However, our genes are clever enough to make it feel like love and babies are programmed to respond to love just as we are programmed to give it. And it's no less wonderful for that.

We talk about "blood" relations, but what we inherit isn't blood, it's genes. Dating right back to our non-human ancestors, our genes have for several million years propelled us towards living in family-based social groups of which the nuclear family was only a part. It's hardly surprising that nowadays this little unit has a hard row to hoe in transforming itself into a free-standing, go-it-alone substitute for the extended family.

23

Nature says that we have a place in our grandchildren's lives We now live in a society where only parents make decisions about their children's upbringing and therefore we may have to accept compromises if we are to take an important part in their lives. Throughout recorded history we find allusions to the special nature of the bond that exists between grandparents and grandchildren, so you and they will benefit enormously if you can keep this little corner of the extended family alive and thriving. And the importance of grandchildren doesn't just apply to babies and young children – a grandparent can be a lifeline for a lonely or disturbed teenager.

Just being a good grandparent is enough

Society and family may have their own views of us but how do we see ourselves? Good, bad or indifferent grandparents?

Don't set your sights too high and bust a gut to be the best granny on the planet. You probably could never be, but by the same token you'll never be the worst either. A realistic point of view will give you that irresistible air of having seen the film through before, of being happy in your skin, of being laid back and relaxed and taking things in your stride. You can easily take on the role of being the still, quiet centre of the storm and, if you're lucky, earn that epithet "Granny knows best".

But thinking that you know best is a very dangerous tack to take, and something you should never allow in your head. You're not a guardian of the truth, you're not a gatekeeper of the family's morals, you're not a world authority on anything, though your opinion may be sought on many issues and found useful if uncritically expressed.

I feel grandparents won't go far wrong if they aim to be their grandchild's and their children's best friend. Then think about how a best friend would behave – to their grandchildren and their children. Not a bossyboots throwing their weight around, but a calm, rational, loving friend.

Thinking that you know best is **a very dangerous tack** *to take and something you should* **never** *allow in your head*

A loving friend Taking on a grandparenting role will be different with each of your children – and stepchildren – and you'll have to be something of a chameleon to tone in to each family set-up. I think I learned some hard lessons when I became a stepmother of two little boys. It was very tough and I felt emotionally bruised a lot of the time until I lowered my sights and decided a worthy approach was simply to try to be their friend. I think this scenario is played out with stepgrandchildren where there isn't a blood tie. There is only a love-tie, which can be just as strong, but you feel you have fewer rights and have to tread carefully. Your stepgrandchildren don't know this; you're their granny and that's what you can be – their most loving friend, possibly even more loving than their "real" granny(s).

These days you may be one of many grandparents. In the family of one of my stepchildren I'm one of four grannies, and three of them are much higher-ranking than I am. I try to know my place in the hierarchy.

But whatever the grown-ups think, the grandchildren will arrive at their own placings: you could be a lowly granny number three or four to the adults but a number one to them. My eldest grandchild, the six-year-old daughter of one my stepsons, gave me a note recently that brought tears to my eyes. It said, *my best granny is Granny Miri.* And if you're lucky you may be invited to be a supernumerary granny. After a communal outing, the small son of one of my daughter-in-law's girlfriends asked if I could be his granny too.

Miriam's mailbag

Q Too young to be a grandma?

My daughter has just told me she's pregnant. This will be my first grandchild and I should be jumping for joy and excitement. Instead, I've just had a good cry because I feel, at 42, I'm much too young to be a grandmother. Just using the word makes me feel old. I feel very guilty because my daughter is ecstatic and I've been pretending I am as happy as she is about the news. Do you think I will get over feeling so miserable inside?

a Your doubts will disappear

Your thinking is a bit skew-whiff at the moment because you're in shock but, trust me, you will get used to being a glamorous grandma. It isn't a requirement of the job that you have to perm your hair, wear a cardi and take up knitting. You'll probably even thank your lucky stars you have the energy and many years ahead of you to enjoy your time with your grandchild. When you hold the tiny baby for the first time I expect all those doubts about being a grandma will disappear.

Keeping up with your grandchild's world

Things are very different now from when you were a child, or even from when you were bringing up your own children. If you keep your role as your grandchild's best friend in your sights, it's easy to see that you should, as any best friend would, keep abreast of what's going on in her world of books, clothes, games, nursery school and later school, music, toys, passions, hobbies, friends, social whirl (the youngest children have dizzying social lives these days), newly acquired skills and interests. As a best friend you only support and cheer, shout hooray and clap your hands with delight. And within a single visit there are numerous opportunities to compliment and praise. Here's one that you can adopt immediately.

I feel grandparents won't go far wrong if they aim to be their grandchild's and their children's **best friend**

I can't remember from whom I learned this trick but it's a great way to encourage your grandchild – and from an early age too. When children learn to speak they first learn *names* and *doing words*. Early examples would be *cat* (a name) and *clap* (a verb). You can praise your grandchild for almost anything if you take the opportunity to focus on praising them for *doing* something, anything. "*Good clapping!*" "*Good crawling!*" "*Good skipping!*" Good everything! Your grandchild comes to know that you're proud of her and she wants to demonstrate her every skill to you because she knows you'll praise her for it.

In fact it's more enriching for you both if you do more than just keeping up with your grandchild's world: you *enter into* your grandchild's world. And you are amply qualified to do that, but most importantly, you have the time to do so, which few parents have on the same scale. It's worth trying to see the world through their eyes, getting inside their heads, and if you can do that you'll get inside their world. I describe it like this because being in their world is a marvellous place to be. You are, and you will feel, special in a way you never have before. And you can become aware as you never have before of sharing something really very special that probably exists quite often between grandparent and grandchild but only comparatively rarely between parent and child.

*It's more enriching for you both if you do **more** than just keeping up with your grandchild's world: **you enter into** your grandchild's world*

Simple is best

Just in case you hold the mistaken belief that being a good grandparent means showering your grandchild with expensive gifts, let me reassure you that it doesn't. Far more important and meaningful to them is that you give them a simple present, then help them play with it or use it; that you get down on the floor and build the farm or the Lego tower and make it easy for your grandchild to let her imagination soar and show off her skills. If your grandchild wants to make a rocket out of a used paper cup, get out the tin foil, the tissue paper, glue and sprinkles and pretend you're both spacemen. She'll play with her paper rocket for longer than her expensive toys because she made it herself with your help and because you made it together.

You can make gifts of joining in games that cost nothing. As one of my granddaughters says, "Come and stand beside me, Granny." Roll up her sleeves, put on her waterproof apron, stand her safely on a chair at the kitchen sink and give her lots of unbreakable jars, bottles, utensils and brushes to pour and wash, clean and fill, empty and refill – play water games together. You can paint together, draw together, scribble together, dig together, plant seeds together, jump in puddles together, shop together (she can pay at the till and wait for your change). All these cost nothing but your time and your caring interest, which are what mean most to a grandchild. To her they feel like love.

2 The special bond

The relationship you can share
with your grandchildren is
indescribable in the terms of any
other. So many qualities are
unique. If you're lucky enough
to be a loving person who loves
babies and respects children
there's a treasure trove of
pleasures waiting for you.

Whoever expected to be falling in love again with each grandchild? Completely besotted with. Totally enamoured of. Overwhelmingly seduced by. Missing the smile, the gurgle, the upward-stretching arms so much it's a physical pain. The constant need to rest your eyes on the face of the beloved. The silly pressing of your lips night, morning and as required through the day to a favourite photograph of the blessed face. The tremulousness that builds as a meeting nears. The racing heart, the dry mouth, the breathlessness as the door opens and into your field of vision floats the adored one.

What babies need

When babies are born they're hot-wired to seek out what for them is an essential vitamin. No, it's not mother's milk, though they do need that. Nor is it love – well, not exactly, though love is essential for their healthy development. It's not touch either, even though baby chimps prefer being touched to being fed, and human babies need lots of touching to thrive.

No, what babies have an unerring radar for is caring interest. Parents have it in spades: all those cuddles, the cooing, baby talk, eye contact, the delight in the faintest response from their baby. Parents alone have it, and only for their baby. Their baby is the caterpillar for their particular leaf.

Parents alone have it – that is, except for grandparents. They, too, have the potential for this caring interest if they give vent to their welling emotions. And if they do, their grandchild beams in, choosing them above all strangers, from very early on and increasingly as they grow up. That's why the grandchild/grandparent relationship can be so special: the grandchild knows with certitude that Granny and

What babies have an unerring ✱ radar for is *caring interest*

Granddad can be relied on in just the same way as Mum and Dad. Indeed sometimes more so, because they feel Granny and Granddad really understand them. And given the perspective of time, Granny and Granddad do understand them in a way that's not possible for Mum and Dad, who are stressed in the ways all young parents are.

So if you're lucky, you find yourself stuck in this virtuous circle with your grandchild and neither of you is inclined to break out of it. A circle where love is unconditional, forgiveness is infinite, interest is endless and communication is heart-baring. There are no no-go areas.

I think this is to do with your conviction of how precious your grandchild is and how precious is every minute spent with him. **So your interest and solicitude, your skills as a teacher, cheerleader and friend can really play out.** And of course you're doing so with the most apt pupil in the world who's dying to excel for you and responds to your praise by growing in self-possession, self-confidence and generosity before your very eyes. And this you can do for your grandchild from the moment he's born.

The special relationship

This belief that your grandchildren are precious means that your relationship with them has a unique character in that it isn't one of adult/child. It's a relationship between equals. Though your grandchild wouldn't know how to describe that character, they absolutely know

♡

what it feels like, as long as you don't crack it wide open by those parental gestures of pulling rank or laying down the law. If you're conscious that it's a relationship between equals, you speak differently. For one thing you automatically avoid that "I" word. Instead, you use the inclusive and infinitely more friendly "we". With one of my grandchildren I had unconsciously been using the magic "we" word in order to encourage her in the form of, "Shall we read a book together?" "Shall we go to the park together?"

Dethronement

Nowhere does the special bond with your grandchild come more into its own than when she's going through the pangs of dethronement. For one reason or other, usually the arrival of a new baby in the family, your grandchild may feel that her position in her parents' affections is being eroded. She feels insecure and needy, and may resort to the kinds of behaviour that she knows will attract her parents' attention. One of the most common is to revert to baby behaviour: so she'll ask to be fed by her parents, she'll want to wear nappies again, she'll want to be nursed like a baby.

Because of your special bond with your grandchild you can give her the attention she's seeking, the extra love that she wants at this tricky time and the reassurance that she requires. You can re-establish her self-confidence and her self-esteem simply with your good grannyship and your ability to give her one-to-one focused attention and fulsome expressions of love.

Imagine my delight when she started to preface (at the age of two) her requests not with the dreaded "I want..." or the imperious "Give me..." but with "Granny, shall we do painting together?", an irresistible way of putting it.

The magic "we" word is invaluable in establishing boundaries, too: "We don't usually throw paper away in the street." Or even stronger, and one I've used successfully with all my grandchildren, " Oh, sorry, we don't do that with Granny" or " We don't speak like that to Granny" or "We do things this way in Granny's house". This approach makes your comments more acceptable to your children as well as to your grandchildren.

Thinking of your grandchildren as precious also means that you're a reliably good listener. You make sure your grandchild knows he has your attention in a way that you probably never had the time or energy for when you were a parent. And you feel quite comfortable play-acting attention and concentration with big gestures (like turning your whole body dramatically to face your grandchild) and following it up theatrically, saying, *"Ooh, please let me see/join in/help you."* Can you imagine how that makes your grandchild feel? He feels as though he's in a spotlight. He can feel the warmth and bask joyfully in it. He thrives in the sunshine of your loving, caring attention.

Is this the strongest bond? So is the bond you share with your grandchild the strongest you'll ever know – almost more than with your own children? Possibly. For starters your focus is somewhat different. With your own child it was almost impossible to separate your concern for them from concerns for yourself. With your grandchild it's different. Your sole focus is the child. Personal considerations hardly figure. In this respect it has the potential to be a more equal relationship, where you forget about yourself and your own sensitivities. It's possible to free yourself from some of the emotions, hang-ups (getting your own way, insisting on a certain kind of discipline, wanting things done in a certain way) you felt you had to enforce with your own children, and which now seem rather pointless. Your grandchild has brought you to a point where ego doesn't matter any more, as you feel able to give all kinds of things away – permissions, routines, rules – that you found so difficult to relinquish as a parent.

As a grandparent you have behind you a *lifetime* of loving

In this way you may find you can give time and love to your grandchildren you regret not giving to your own children. But don't recriminate. Don't wish you could turn the clock back and do it all over again. One of the reasons that you're so well equipped to give your grandchildren the time and caring attention you couldn't give your own children is because you have behind you a lifetime of loving. You've reached a point where your love can be very grown-up and very generous. But you have had to graduate to this point, so to speak. Loving your own children was one of the steps along the way.

You're emotionally mature this time around Because your emotions are so different this time around, you can watch the interactions of the whole family in a slightly more detached way, from a distance. This means you can be especially useful in difficult situations – say, in a battle between sibling grandchildren and a single other. You have no parental bias, you favour no one. So you can take on the comforter role for the child who is most upset without entering into arguments about whose fault it originally was, without making justifications for bad behaviour and without doling out punishments. In this way you're a very useful peacemaker. Your concern is for the distressed child and you need not – indeed it's best if you don't – make judgements about rights and wrongs. You're neutral, outside of the family friction, and you're able to give cuddles, kind words and consolation to a child who needs those things but might not get them were you absent.

Also, by concentrating your attentions on the child you avoid the pitfall of being drawn into discussions about fault and blame – always best avoided, because sensitive parents (your children, stepchildren and children-in-law) may construe your comments as criticism; the next thing you know family relationships are strained, or worse, you become estranged from your children.

So if you always concentrate on your grandchild and put him first you'll avoid drawing attention to any supposed deficiencies of parenting. And those, it should be added, may only reflect your point of view and not anyone else's.

It seems grandmas are special

Researchers have identified what they call "good grandmothers", perhaps those who have a natural love and inclination towards babies and young children. These natural grandmothers identify with the parent and are happy to be an assistant mother and helper, while acting with great tenderness and understanding to their grandchildren. What's not always realized and understood is that grandparents can

What if you don't feel grandmother love?

My emphasis on this especially loving bond that can exist between grandparent and grandchild may strike you as a bit over the top. There are some people who don't feel the joy of grandparenting to the same extent that I do; their feelings may be not so much in technicolour as in sepia or monochrome.

If you're one of those people who doesn't engage readily with children and babies, it's possible that you won't with your grandchildren either. It may be that you gave so much love and concern to your children that you have nothing left and perhaps you've exhausted your supply of love by the time you become a grandparent. Grandparenthood may feel a little foreign to you and there's nothing wrong with that, though there's plenty of research to show that a rich relationship with a grandparent greatly benefits a grandchild in many different ways.

play a positive, effective, supportive and worthwhile role *in the development* of their grandchildren. Grandparents can soften an intense relationship between parent and child, allowing the child freedom to develop healthily. So an interested, caring, thoughtful and mature person who's directly involved in the family has great potential for helping the development of their grandchildren. The wise intervention of a grandparent with objectivity and distance can give a beneficial consistency, warmth and balance to a family and the atmosphere within it.

This special sense of harmony which grandparents can confer with the avoidance of conflict has been shown to have a positive effect in heading off childhood behaviour problems. On the other hand, hostility by a grandparent to a grandchild can result in the opposite and lead to antisocial behaviour in a child or adolescent. The potential contributions of grandparents to grandchildren in terms of accumulated experience are vast, especially if, as the grandparents grow older, they continue to grow in sweetness and serenity and see grandparenthood as the final validation of their lives (though I'd be first to admit this isn't always the case).

A role model for your own children

We should all probably recognize that how we handle our grandparenting reflects how we solved many earlier difficulties in relating to our own children and, in turn, this will probably influence their own children's relationship to them as grandparents. Possibly one of the most important aspects of being a good grandparent is that you're acting as a role model for your own children when they reach that stage of their lives.

How we act with our children when we become grandparents influences how they accept us getting older right across the board. It offers us the chance of accepting and going through a stage of our lives when we have significant value and which is gratifying for us and them. We give our children the opportunity to learn how to enjoy good relations with their children. This is all part of the capacity which grandparents have to "give back" to society, but especially to their families, using their experience and their knowledge in practical and creative ways. Grandparents also have the role, so well played out for us by matriarchal elephants and whales, of preserving and transmitting cultural and family knowledge through the generations – a history that invariably fascinates grandchildren.

Do we have a need to be grandparents? Becoming a grandparent is an opportunity for growth and many people don't want to miss out on it. It's gratifying to have influence and significance, and that's hard to turn your back on. Grandparents often fulfil the role of parents and welcome it. Nonetheless, the role of grandparent has its own responsibilities and rewards of a unique and positive kind. The delicacy and tact of a grandparent is a valuable model for worthwhile attitudes and behaviour. The refinements of a grandparent's emotional expression act as a buffer within the family and provide a unique opportunity for a child to learn many different ways of reacting to unusual situations and of using leisure time gainfully.

Grandchildren may seek you out as a parent There are many situations in which grandparents serve as parents. Often they are sought by desperate grandchildren in search of security; often the surrogate roles of the grandparents aren't recognized for their added value. Children aren't only interested in relatives who bring gifts. Sometimes, when parents die, grandparents can give a measure of security to the children, who may be adolescents or young adults, security that can't be given by other members of the family and is much more effective than that given by a stranger.

The presence of grandparents, if often not recognized as a substitute for the absent parent, may ward off a serious psychological reaction to the trauma of separation. The unique quality that a grandparent offers to a child who has lost one or both parents is a stable relationship with cherished memories; ties that don't exist with anyone else. And in some cultures – for instance, Native Americans – children persistently seek contact with their grandparents; if a biological grandparent isn't available, another older member of the community is adopted for the role. It would seem that children have a profound need for grandparents.

There's a difference between being a parent and being a grandparent

Only grief lies ahead if you confuse these two roles. Grandparents are not a grandchild's parents, and behaving as if they are will lead to trouble. There's more about this in chapters three and four, but in general I'm a firm believer that parents know what's best for their children and have to be given the freedom to bring up their children as they think fit. I'd even go as far as saying they have to be allowed to make their own mistakes, which may be painful for you to sit by and watch.

But remember you've had your turn. You've had your go at bringing up a family, and I'm sure you've learned from experience and wished you'd done things differently. Your children have the right to the

*Grandparents are **not** a grandchild's parents, and behaving as if they are will **lead to trouble***

same thing. Your role is not to bring up your grandchildren unless, of course, you've been specifically entrusted with that role or find it thrust upon you. Encourage good habits by all means with praise and reward and try to play down bad ones, but you're overstepping the mark if you think laying down the law falls within your aegis.

Positive feedback At the very least it's insulting to your child and their spouse if you think they need parenting lessons from you. There may be areas where you think their approach needs fine-tuning, but it would be wiser to wait until asked than to jump in and undermine their confidence. If you chip away at their confidence, and I know that there are times when you can barely stop yourself from doing so, it will be construed as interfering and you'll lose their trust. It takes one small step to destroy their trust and it's a mountain almost too high to climb to regain it. Instead, I've found it's best to channel that critical energy into positive feedback.

Even if you can hardly keep yourself in check, look for ways in which your son is a great father and your daughter-in-law is a fantastic mother. And then say so. And there are a million ways in which they are. Concentrate on those. I have to admit that hearing my daughter-in-law say, "Thanks, Miri..." when I compliment her on her qualities as a mother is one of the sweetest sounds I know, and I want to hear her say it again and again.

Remember, your children and their partners are feeling insecure to begin with. They're only too aware of their failings and weaknesses. They don't need you to point them out. But they do need reassurance that they're doing a good job, and support for making a difficult decision. Those things aren't hard to give if you're alert to your children's needs.

Keeping in touch

Your special relationship feeds on contact, but that may not always be easy. You may live at the opposite end of the country from your children and only see them and your grandchildren maybe once or twice a year on special occasions. Remember, it's as important – if not more important – for your grandchildren to hear from you as it is for you to hear from them and there are lots of ways to do that.

- Telephone calls – if your grandchild has a mobile phone, call her on that so it's just the two of you.
- Learn to text and text her now and then with news and questions about herself.
- Send letters, postcards, birthday cards, photos.
- If you don't already use it, master doing email just for her.
- Buy a digital camera and email your favourite photos with your own commentary.
- Buy her a camera so she can do the same.
- Ask her to download a selection of her favourite music for you.
- Invest in a webcam so that you can see one another while you talk "face to face".
- You'll inevitably see more of your grandchildren if you travel to them, so make the effort. It really is too much hassle for your children and your grandchildren always to travel to your house.

43

Where do grandfathers fit in?

If you're a granddad reading this book I'd understand if you felt overlooked, and while I'm keen on grandparents irrespective of gender, I'd have to say my emphasis on grandmothers stems from two disparate sources.

The first is the precedent in the animal kingdom. It isn't a large, loving, patriarchal bull elephant who guards his females and protects their young. No, the bull elephants are off doing their own thing at the first stirrings of sexual maturity. And it isn't the male whale who keeps the school secure and thriving.

The second is closer to home. In my experience it's rarely grandpa who initiates contact with the grandchildren. Indeed it may be quite the opposite. He has to be cajoled into visits and outings. Once he's with his grandchildren it's often a different matter, but not usually until they're of an age to relate well to adults. Grandpas tend to come into their own when grandchildren reach the age of six or seven.

In fact, for older children the grandpa/grandchild relationship can be just as rich and special as that with grandma. The only problem is that it probably doesn't have the history, because granny, of course, has been forming her relationship with her grandchildren since birth. So grandpas can have quite a lot of catching up to do. Maybe it's the same as with fathers and small babies. Men frequently feel shut out from the early stages of the baby's life, and mothers aren't always as inclusive as they might be. Perhaps grannies aren't either.

There's an Italian proverb that goes: if nothing is going well, call your grandmother.

You'll be nearing perfection as a grandparent if your children think: if nothing is going well, call mum/mother-in-law.

It can be a two-way street There are a lot of things going for "good" grandparents – grandchildren seek you out and parents recognize your enormous usefulness and value. They also come to see that your bond with their children, the grandparent/grandchild bond, is undeniably a good thing for everyone, including them. So while on the one hand you're anxious not to upset the parents, they, on the other, are equally anxious not to upset you. You have become too important to their baby and, as a result, to them. You've become a valued and respected member of the family team and you'll find that they, as well as you, start to practise restraint.

If this mutual respect for each other grows you'll find your opinion is frequently sought and you'll be left to do things your way. This first happened to me one evening when I was babysitting and I asked what I should give my grandchild for supper. "Oh, just choose something from the fridge." And bedtime? "Whenever you think." Does she need a bath? "You judge."

If nothing is going well,
call your grandmother

Loving advice

One afternoon I arrived to visit one of my families of grandchildren to find that my middle granddaughter, Beth, had had a bad day at school. She'd been taken to the headmistress after a tantrum and thrown a second in the street. At tea she behaved badly with her cousin and there were tears all round. When her mother arrived home everyone was upset and she asked for my take on the situation. I usually try to avoid getting in the middle of family problems, but realized I could help here. I thought about it and the next day emailed my daughter-in-law the following response, which was very well received. This showed me that sometimes it is worth giving an opinion, as long as it is carefully considered and offered with love rather than bossiness.

(Some background on this – Beth's elder sister is learning to read and has one-on-one practice with Mum or Dad every evening. Her new baby sister of four months is a star and charms everyone.)

My response:

Darling, it was great to see you both last night and to spend a few hours with your enchanting girls. I love and admire you hugely. I've been thinking about our adorable Beth and I want to reassure you. This might help.

Tantrums at this age are natural when ambition exceeds talent. Also, Beth is in the throes of middle-child syndrome and all middle children suffer this. It's especially hard when your elder sister is so talented – it's well-nigh intolerable for a three-year-old to have talent above and a star below. She's feeling an unavoidable sense of dethronement, which we can certainly help with.

Here's what she's not:

- She's not especially naughty – I'd avoid that construct altogether. It isn't useful or helpful.
- She isn't basically unhappy.

Here's what she is:

- She's seeking reassurance of her importance.
- She's reacting to a difficult situation in the only way she knows how.
- She's demanding attention in the form of tantrums because it is the only tool a three-year-old has.

Here's what I suggest:

- All can be put right by one-on-one attention. Daddy is pivotal in all this (you're her mummy, she's always got you).
- Daddy must give Beth (and any child in this situation) ONE HALF DAY (at the weekend) of uninterrupted focused attention. Tantrums will stop in two weeks if this regime can be managed.
- Here's the hardest thing – leave her alone, as long as she's safe, when she's having a tantrum. So that she learns they don't work.

Please ignore all of the above if I'm being an old busybody. I just don't want you to beat yourself up when one, you're a fantastic mum; and two, you're better at keeping so many balls in the air than anyone I've ever met. You have my unconditional support and I'm here at any time.

3 Golden rules
for grandparents

Most grandparents who write to me with a problem believe right is on their side. One of my aims in this chapter is to debunk the idea that grandparents, as an older and wiser generation, can impose their will on a younger, less experienced generation. That way lies disaster. But mainly I'd like to help you be a well-loved grandparent who is welcome to see your grandchildren as often as you wish.

It's as well to remember that we're all grandparents by invitation, not by divine right. Your role as a grandparent will be easier if you have respect for your children's right to bring up their children as they see fit. If you espouse this approach it's easier to understand that interference and criticism are counterproductive, as is undermining your children's authority and that of their partner. It's also death to your relationship if you make a habit of criticizing your grandchildren, because your children, quite reasonably, will take it as criticism of their ability to be good parents; it's also extremely unkind to your grandchildren. It's wise to let your actions be guided by the knowledge that your children could, if it ever came to it, exercise the ultimate sanction and stop you seeing your grandchildren.

Ten golden rules for good grandparenting

1 Visit only by invitation or mutual arrangement
2 Keep communication open at all costs
3 Respect your children's boundaries
4 Praise your children on being good parents
5 Keep a well-developed sense of fairness and humour
6 Never undermine your children or your grandchildren
7 Offer support and advice without always expecting it to be accepted
8 Resist the temptation to get embroiled in emotional blackmail
9 Be a grandparent who's nice to know
10 Look for "chinks" only you can fill

1 Visit only by invitation or mutual arrangement

What you're striving for is to be heartily welcomed every time you arrive to spend time with your children and grandchildren rather than greeted by a muttered aside, "Your mother's here again". You're there by invitation, but it would be wrong – and unfair – if you acted like a visitor. You're not. You're a member of the family, so it's far better to put on the kettle and ask if anyone would like a cup of tea than wait to be offered one and have your child or your in-law make it for you. You know where the cups, tea and milk are kept and it will be appreciated if you make yourself useful.

Often the payback for having the freedom to see your grandchildren is that you offer to travel to them. This may be inconvenient, but it will be much more popular than an invitation for your children, babies and impedimenta to travel to you. Yours may be a trying, trashing journey but theirs is definitely more so. Added to which, your children may feel they have to stand on ceremony and behave well when visiting you, whereas at their house anything goes. It's much more relaxing for all of you. And as you're not on home ground it just might remind you to put your best foot forwards, which is no bad thing.

A visit with a purpose It helps if your visit has a purpose: you're bringing a present, you're helping at a grandchild's birthday party, you're showing your daughter or daughter-in-law how to use her new sewing machine. I remember when one of my daughters-in-law was attempting to knit the layette for her expected baby and she got in a muddle. "Miri, can you knit?", she asked. "Could you sort this out for me?" It was a full 35 years since I had knitted, but as I took the needles and the wool it all came back, and my offer to knit a few inches was readily taken up. "God, mum," said my son, "I didn't know you could knit!" (Thinks: there all kinds of things you don't know, my lad, but I'll bide my time.)

Once there, you'll score points if you join in and help with whatever needs doing without getting in the way. Don't sit and wait to be asked. Be ready to unload the dishwasher, wash and dry a few dishes or lay the table. Offer to make your grandchildren's tea or take them off to play with the toy you bought them. Suggest playtime in the garden with balls, bats, bicycles, tricycles or trampoline so that your grandchildren can show off their skills to you while your children enjoy a few moments of peace and quiet. You'll be the family favourite if you're always willing to read books to your grandchildren and do baths and bedtimes.

Be a hands-on helper If you have the strength and stamina you can take this supporting role even further and be a hands-on helper with some of the boring daily routines all parents find onerous. If you're a driver and have access to a car, you could do the school pick-up so mum doesn't have to rush home from work or shopping. You could take your grandchildren to another child's party while the parents do something more productive. You could find information for them on the Internet that they haven't the time to search for. A half-day trip at the weekend would take your grandchildren off their parents' hands so that they can get some jobs done. If you have the expertise to do jobs around the house that they can never get round to and irritate them to death, you'll be a star, easing their burden while giving you time with your grandchildren.

Never arrive empty-handed. It doesn't have to be a special gift – just a sheet of stickers, a book, a bag of marbles or a paper aeroplane kit. And a cake for tea would be good.

While you're talking to each other everything can be changed. While you're estranged nothing can be

Golden rules for grandparents

2 Keep communication open at all costs

As a grandparent you'll need the judgement of Solomon and the patience of Job. Remember, you need your children and grandchildren emotionally more than they need you, so you have to make all the running, and that seems to me to be as it should be. You're older and wiser. It's your responsibility to be the peacemaker, not theirs, even if something they've done has hurt you terribly. When your pride pricks you, just consider – would you rather stay aloof and alone than offer the olive branch and be included again? To my mind it's a no-brainer. My children didn't have to be that old for me to realize that no matter how difficult relations might become between us, continuing to have a dialogue with them was paramount to me. I've written that I would crawl on my hands and knees over broken glass to keep the channels of communication open, and that about sums it up. While you're talking to each other everything can be changed. While you're estranged nothing can be.

I'm not suggesting it's easy. Far from it. You may have to make all sorts of adjustments, concessions and sacrifices which will cost you dearly. But they've got to be worth it. Just consider the alternative – no, it's unthinkable. You may have to be more self-critical than you've ever been before. You may have to admit you have faults you'd rather

✳

53

not concede. You may have to change the way you think and behave. That's not a bad thing either. Becoming a grandparent is an opportunity to grow, and that's an offer we can't refuse. Just try making the first overture. You'll be astonished how good it makes you feel. And your children will love you for it.

3 Respect your children's boundaries

I'm sure there were times when you resented your parents' interference or heavy-handedness when you were bringing up your children. I know I did. I imagine you wished they'd mind their own business. You might even have said (or at least thought), "If, as you say, I'm making a terrible mistake and I will live to regret it, I still have the right to make my own mistakes."

I remember even facing off my mother. One of my four little boys had been naughty and she was pressing me to punish him, saying, "If you don't, he'll never learn that he mustn't do that" (whatever it was). My mother and I had diametrically opposed views about punishment: I believed in teaching by reward, she believed in punishment. I also believed, and still do, that every child has the right to go to sleep happy, not weeping about some past misdemeanour, and I firmly told her so and to butt out, so to speak.

Becoming a grandparent is an
opportunity to grow,
and that's an offer we can't refuse

New ways

Here are a couple of examples of my recent experiences as a grandmother. When my granddaughter was three months old my son, who's a hands-on dad, told me that he and my daughter-in-law wanted to try a new way of settling her at night. He explained that they knew it would be hard for me, but please, would I go along with it? I did, and this meant I sat outside her room listening to her crying, my heart breaking. **But they were right**. We successfully weaned her off being nursed to sleep, and it only took four nights

Fast forward two years. This time my son said, "Mum, I don't want to give you orders, but this is an order. She goes to bed at 7pm, no matter how many books you want to read her". (Bedtime had been slipping to 7:30/8:00pm.) **They were right again**. The broken nights stopped and my granddaughter slept for twelve hours.

So if you feel your point of view should carry more weight than your children's, think again. It could be that you're just plain out of date. Your children are in a different world, following modern childcare guidelines on such matters as weaning and sleep patterns, and your old rules of thumb have been passé for decades. Better to bone up on the latest theories so that you can swap ideas as equals.

You're really asking for trouble if you flout their wishes, thinking that you know best and hoping they won't find out. Believe me, you will be found out. And you won't have a leg to stand on. You may find yourself on the wrong end of an argument with your children from

Miriam's mailbag

Q Isn't she doing it all wrong?

I've just said goodbye to my daughter and son-in-law, who came to stay over Christmas with my three-year-old grandson and one-year-old granddaughter, and I'm so upset.

At mealtimes my son-in-law would say to the boy, "Do you want this or do you want mine?", distracting his attention from the meal. He let my grandson leave the table and come back when he wanted and, of course, when he saw our puddings he didn't want his dinner! Also, instead of saying, "It's bedtime", my son-in-law would say, "It's time to go upstairs," resulting in tantrums before he eventually went to bed. My grandson doesn't seem to have any guidelines for good behaviour. They even let the baby walk around drinking out of a bottle. They never sit her down to drink.

My husband was very firm with our three children, but my daughter is adamant she's going to raise her son and daughter her way. Surely her ways are wrong?

a Granny doesn't always know best

It's time for you to relax and be more laid-back. Do you really believe you raised perfect children with your own methods? Even if this were true, you have absolutely no right to interfere in any way with how your grandchildren are being raised. To be at ease with your daughter and her children, you must accept your childrearing days are over and it's not your responsibility to set standards.

In any case, I don't know why you're worrying about the way your grandson eats his meals. The world isn't going to stop if he doesn't sit nicely at the table with his knife and fork, or settle down without a murmur to go to bed. Raising children isn't supposed to be trouble-free, and every generation has its own ideas on the best way to go about it.

As a grandparent and mother-in-law you're walking a tightrope. And the easiest way to fall out with the young ones is to question their parenting skills. In your shoes, I'd be inclined to keep my opinions to myself. They probably think they're raising the children appropriately and would hate to have interference from you.

There are developmental reasons why children between one and three peck and poke at their food. After a year of rapid growth, during which the average one-year-old triples his birth weight, toddlers gain weight more slowly. So, of course, they need less food. And always being on the go also affects their eating patterns. They don't sit still for anything, even food. Snacking their way though the day is more compatible with these busy explorers' lifestyles than sitting down to a fully fledged feast. Toddlers should graze.

Look at your grandchildren and see if they've the stamina to get through the day's play. Are they happy? If they're always going to a doctor to see what's wrong with them, only then may you have a genuine cause for concern. Granny doesn't always know best.

which you can't escape. It's humiliating, but much worse, you will have lost their trust. Things will never be the same. You've burned your boats, and for what? For a momentary triumph.

A successful role as grandparent means putting yourself last. Your views only count if solicited. Ego has no value in grandparenting. You have a longer perspective, you're sensitive to the needs of others. Your ego has evolved. Put that on display.

A good guideline is to get sign-off from your children on everything. Ask them if something you want to do is OK. Compromise if necessary. This way you engender trust rather than destroy it. Another way of putting it is FIT IN. Accept your children's ways of doing things. As a grandparent you're a team member, not a team leader.

4 Praise your children on being good parents

I may be lucky, but all of my children, stepchildren and sons- and daughters-in-law are great parents. Every time I see them I watch them doing things I didn't do with my own children and wish I had. I see them being more patient, more child-friendly, more understanding than I ever was. I watch my grandchildren respond with delight and happiness as my children encourage, help, show, act out in a manner that never occurred to me. They are light years ahead of where I was.

That's not to say that now and then I don't think they might do the odd thing differently, but why dwell on that when there are so many positives to concentrate on? It's a bit like a marriage: there are seven out of ten things about your partner that you adore and three things out of ten that drive you mad. But you concentrate on the seven out of ten. It's neither useful nor productive to do otherwise. It's the same with your children's parenting skills.

Now, again like telling your partner you love them whenever you think it, tell your children how much you admire them whenever you notice their doing something that only a good parent would do. This reinforcement is the bricks and mortar of friendship and trust, and you'll find both will flower under your tender loving care.

Defer to the parents Another good habit to cultivate is to defer to your children when your grandchild asks your permission for something – another biscuit, or to get out the paints, paper, apron and do painting. It's so easy to say, "If Mummy (or Daddy) thinks it's OK, that's fine". It's also reassuring for your children and gratifying for your grandchildren to hear you say, "Wasn't that clever of Daddy", or "Good job, Mummy". It's a really bonding mannerism to cultivate.

Your skills as a communicator may be sorely tried if something happens between you and your children that has the potential to be really divisive and possibly ruin your relationship forever. Instead of taking up the moral high ground you can decide to support your child through thick and thin. That way, if things ever get really bad they will turn to you. You're there to pick up the pieces; you aren't there to smash china. If you're big enough to do that, your children will be grateful and loving back for as long as you live.

I see my children being **more** *patient,* **more** *child-friendly,* **more** *understanding than I ever was*

Miriam's mailbag

Q Why is my niece is getting all the attention?

My sister and I were pregnant at the same time. I was first to go into labour and had a beautiful baby boy, my second son. A week later my sister gave birth to her first baby, a beautiful baby girl. Since then, my mum seems to have forgotten the existence of her new grandson and his brother. She's been cooing over the little princess while my two princes are hardly getting a look-in. I know it's petty but I can't help feeling annoyed and upstaged. How do I keep my temper while my niece receives all the attention?

a Grandma loves them all

I doubt your mum is deliberately playing favourites. You're simply up against the novelty factor and an accident of timing. If there had been a few more weeks in between arrivals, I'm sure your newborn would have had the centre stage. She's now got her very first granddaughter so it's hardly surprising she's thrilled to bits. It doesn't mean she loves your two any less. Your son isn't going to be emotionally scarred because he received a few less cuddles from grandma, so do your best to be philosophical and enjoy this opportunity to have your son all to yourself.

5 Keep a well-developed sense of fairness and humour

Even with your own children you probably had a favourite, one who seemed closer to you than the others, one who seemed to understand you better and you felt loved you more than the others. You may find the same thing with your grown-up family, which expands when your children marry and, possibly, if you remarry and your partner has children of their own.

But it would be wrong if you openly showed any favouritism, especially towards your grandchildren. Within your own family of children, favouritism was on a small stage and you could contain it. Within your expanded, grown-up family it's on a big stage, thrown into relief by the spotlight of their insecurities and jealousies, possibly even by their jockeying for position and status.

You have to be the still, quiet centre of the family, guided by a keen sense of justice and even-handedness. If possible, you need to nip in the bud bad feelings that, if left unchecked, may suddenly erupt, to everyone's cost.

Favouritism is painful I receive many letters from children who are wounded by a grandparent's favouritism for, say, a sibling's children who seem to get more attention, more treats, bigger and more expensive presents. And it's natural for them to feel slighted. Their pain is a mixture of sadness for their overlooked children and resentment that a sibling is getting special treatment.

Of course, it helps if your sense of humour is always near the surface. As in almost any difficult situation, humour can defuse all the tension in a family disagreement. You're fortunate if you can see the funny side of things, make light of problems and accidents, and defuse unhappiness with a little joke.

6 Never undermine your children or your grandchildren

There can be little more demoralising for a young mother than a sniffy grandparent who lives by the mantra, "I always found it worked better if...". Now this person is no doubt kind (they have tried to find a polite way of expressing their view) and well-meaning (they're drawing on a lifetime of experience from which they're convinced you'll benefit). But how much more acceptable their comment would be if phrased, "What a useful way of doing that. I never thought of it". The first undermines, the second praises. If you run down the efforts of your children you'll be disliked and will be shown the door. You'd hesitate to run down your best friend; why your children?

It seems odd that grandparents feel they have the right to poormouth their children and children-in-law, but they do. They will find that distance, separation and estrangement may be the result, and there'll be no one to blame but themselves. It's even worse to bring down your grandchildren, who are vulnerable to all criticism and defenceless to your unkind words. Nothing is more calculated to make you a very unpopular grandparent than picking fault with your grandchildren. Parents get defensive because they feel under fire and, even worse, your unkind words can reduce a child to tears or destroy self-confidence. To do either of these things – criticize parents or criticize grandchildren – covertly behind your children's backs is worst of all. It always gets back to them and your name will be mud, I'm afraid.

You'd hesitate to run down your best friend; why your children?

Miriam's mailbag

Q What can I do about my mum? She finds fault with me in front of my children

My mum has always interfered in my life. I don't enjoy being around her, and I often find myself making excuses for her not to visit. She's always finding fault and totally undermines me in front of my two little girls, aged eight and eleven. In her eyes I can't do anything right. I do have enough faith in myself to disagree with her view of me, but it still doesn't stop me from feeling hurt. The problem is my girls love their grandma and like seeing her.

a Let her know that this constant criticism is out of order

Our nearest and dearest always have the greatest capacity to hurt us, and it seems your mum has been attempting to control you for years. Being your mum doesn't give her the right to treat you with such disrespect. It's high time you let her know that her constant criticism is out of order and you're no longer going to accept it. Explain that unless she can make a genuine effort to change her attitude and behaviour, she will no longer be welcome in your home.

Perhaps her devotion to her grandchildren will motivate her to examine her conduct, because it isn't in their interest either to spend time with a woman who's so controlling and scornful.

7 Offer support and advice without always expecting it to be accepted

If you offer advice tonelessly to a disinterested third party you wouldn't automatically expect them to take it. You'd expect them to consider it dispassionately and make their own decision. This, if you can manage it, is how to offer advice (when sought) to your grown-up children. If you expect little, as often as not, you'll be pleasantly surprised.

The point about offering advice tonelessly rather than emphatically is that you give your children the space to weigh up what you've said, without feeling their backs are against the wall. As reasonable people, they'll probably realize the wisdom of your advice and, given the space, take it – at least in part.

Financial support doesn't mean you can dictate how *your money is spent*

The same tonelessness applies to any financial support you may give your children, too. For some of us, reaching grandparenthood means that you have the funds to pay for all kinds of things and services your children need. I'm not an advocate of keeping your estate intact, then passing it on to your children at a time when, most likely, they're out of the financial woods. I think it is often a better idea to give it away when your children are of an age when they need help to buy their first house, a car or a foreign holiday, when a leg-up really is enabling for them. But, by the same token, this doesn't mean that you have the right to veto their chosen house or disapprove of the type of car they want. Financial support doesn't mean you can dictate how your money is spent.

8 Resist the temptation to get embroiled in emotional blackmail

As someone who is part of the family but has the perspective to be an objective observer, it's easy to find yourself called upon by two warring factions to give your support. You may even find your loyalties are split in two. Perhaps you can see some sense on both sides. Or you may find your blood tie is unfairly outweighing your support for an in-law, despite yourself. Before you know it, the situation can escalate and you find yourself with impossibly difficult choices to make. You may even feel hamstrung to make any choice for fear of upsetting the parents of your grandchildren, thereby losing contact with them, the situation you most dread.

Coming between parents in this kind of emotional tug-of-war is dangerous. There's no question that the mother of your grandchildren, whether she's your daughter, your daughter-in-law or your step-daughter, holds all the trump cards and, while your heart may yearn to support your son, your son-in-law or your stepson-in-law, it's courting disaster to come out and nail your colours to the mast. And it would be quite wrong to do so. Disagreements between your children and their husbands and wives are none of your business. Furthermore, you'll probably never get it right, but always end up upsetting someone. Loyalties may also be tested if you have a new partner and find yourself torn between him or her and your children's families.

Don't take sides By far the best policy is to refrain from taking sides, if necessary by leaving the room, keeping quiet, going out for a walk. Never come between husband and wife or you'll be seen as a troublemaker and be unwelcome. Make sure your behaviour reflects this neutrality. Quite often body language, a look, a murmur can show your true feelings and bring down a fragile house of cards.

I'd rarely say so, but grandparents may find their own interests are best served by sitting on the fence. An even better strategy may be to say that you can see merits on both sides and then quickly to add something along the lines of, "Whatever you decide is fine with me – you can count on my support".

9 Be a grandparent who's nice to know

People who are optimistic live longer, so if you can spread a little of your optimism around your family you'll always be welcome and live to enjoy that. There are some people who naturally look on the bright side and make little of adversity; my mother was one of them. I remember her encouraging my sister and me with epithets like *every cloud has a silver lining* and *a trouble shared is a trouble halved*.

We love being with people who take a positive approach to life and it's never more valuable than from a grandparent. After all, with your experience, saying you think things aren't too bad is testament indeed, and everyone will feel reassured. It's also good for your grandchildren to grow up seeing you as a role model who makes light of problems and difficulties. You can help give them an idea of what really matters and what isn't that important. In doing so you downscale what could turn into a crisis and reassure them that all will be well – and with your positive intervention, it will.

It's wonderful to be useful and to be needed and **if you're nice to know** *you will be*

Be positive Like any good friend you can accentuate the positive and eliminate the negative for your children and grandchildren. Looking on the bright side is a great gift to give your family, and if you come to be seen as a problem-solver, if you can be relied on as someone who makes things easier rather than more difficult, someone who will step into the breach, you will be enfolded into your children's families.

The stage you're at in your life equips you perfectly for this role. You have all the skills, honed from a lifetime of overcoming obstacles and dealing with adversity. You know the solution to most problems because you've seen the film through many times before. And if you're a compassionate counsellor and don't throw your weight around, you'll find your children come to you again and again for your problem-solving skills. This two-way appreciation of each other is exactly what you need as you get older. It's wonderful to be useful and to be needed and if you're nice to know you will be.

Then there's all that love you have to draw upon and which is so appealing to your children and your grandchildren. Just yesterday I heard one of my sons say "...and Mum lovingly changed her diary around so she could cover for us...". Lovingly. That word came as a surprise. And of course your grandchildren are just as appreciative if you can be their grand comforter of all ills, reliably ready with consoling words and reassuring cuddles. You can make all their pain, hurt and insecurity vanish with a kiss and a hug. They learn they can rely on you to be ready with gentleness and understanding at any time because they know you want to relieve their distress and mend the situation. You brighten their sadness with a smile and a comforting "There, there," rather than heighten it with a frown and a scolding.

10 Look for "chinks" only you can fill

This is where you could come into your own as a grandparent by putting your own distinctive stamp on your role.

By a "chink" I mean an activity (like gardening) or a hobby (bird watching) or a skill (perhaps drawing), which gives your grandchildren the opportunity of accompanying you into a world of your own. The special quality of a chink is that you have boundless enthusiasm for it. You communicate that energy to your grandchildren so that it becomes a thrilling journey you undertake together, with you as benevolent teacher and your grandchild as willing student.

If you start this off when your grandchild is very young, say two years old, she'll grow up thinking of you as an exciting companion. Children are very sensitive to this act of joyful discovery and as soon as they're able, they start to bring little gifts of that same kind to you. You form your own virtuous circle, where you respect what each can teach the other, and it will probably last for life.

And of course you open up your grandchild's world in a way that's unique, to something that his parents have neither the time nor the experience for. It can be anything from finding out about insects to stamp collecting or jewellery-making – the possibilities are endless – but it's the doing it together that counts.

Miriam's mailbag

Q Should I keep my children away from their bad-tempered granddad?

On more than one occasion, my father-in-law has been brusque with our two children aged six and three. He shouts if they get in his way, or says they're too noisy. The children are frightened of him, which I think is very sad. My own dad is dead so he's their only granddad. My mother-in-law's a completely different story. She adores the children and goes out of her way to make them feel special and loved. I hate putting them in the firing line of his bad temper, but if I limit contact I'll be depriving them of their grandmother. What should I do?

a Keep him happy if you can

You can't change granddad and if you sever ties with him, I agree you'll make your mother-in-law very unhappy, which wouldn't be fair to her or the children. You might give some thought to protecting him from the children to minimize his angry outbursts. Accept he'll never understand, and whatever they can do to conform to his way of living, while he's around, will help. Colouring books, drawing and reading are all quiet activities. Ideally keep him in the family if you can, because although he may not be a great granddad for them at this age, he may mellow as they get older. Could your husband say something tactful and apologetic to his mother?

4 Sensitive issues

In all other areas of your life you may be a free agent, but where your grandchildren are concerned I'm not sure that you are. Your love for them may be so great that you find yourself held hostage to that love, willingly or unwillingly, and nowhere more so than on subjects where you don't see eye to eye with your children.

On sensitive issues your guiding principle should be that if you upset your children or your children-in-law, you might lose access to your grandchildren. If you sense an impending rift, remember that your children hold all the cards. In this chapter I've covered what seem to me to be the most common problems, and there's kind of a hierarchy of sensitivity, going from sensitive to tricky to frankly no-go areas that are too sensitive to broach, or that you broach at your peril.

The role of grandparent has, like that of parent, to be learned. We can rely on our instincts for general guidelines, but on specifics it's as though we need to serve an apprenticeship. If we fail to appreciate this, mistakes get made. If we accept our mistakes, admit to them and apologize, their impact can be assuaged. You won't go far wrong if you're never slow to say sorry.

Try for discretion, tolerance and flexibility

In my experience, rifts can occur right across families as well as up and down generations. For instance, two sets of grandparents may not see eye to eye or get along. One set may give or get more time and attention, so jealousy may develop, resentments build and some disagreements erupt. As the bottom line is access to your grandchildren, it's wise to practise, if you can, discretion, tolerance and flexibility. Be a kind and conciliatory arbitrator; don't risk losing contact.

Some emotions, which all too easily surface when sensitive issues arise, are not at all useful or helpful. Even though you have to make a superhuman effort, they are best kept under control. In truth, they're best kept under control in all areas of our lives, but if you remember how high the stakes are where your children and grandchildren are concerned, that superhuman effort is all the more worth making.

You won't go far wrong if you're never slow to *say sorry*

If you can manage it you can be a chief helper to all the family. Your mantra should be "Granny will help" not "Granny will throw a spanner in the works". In this way you can assume the role of teacher and arbiter to your grandchildren. And you can teach them gentleness, thoughtfulness, kindness, generosity – and tidiness and cleanliness if you like – simply by example, without imposing oppressive rules. Instead of laying down the law, use the words, "We usually do this" and "We don't usually do that", using the "we" to include yourself and make it easy for your grandchildren to accept.

This may strike you as overly self-effacing, even sacrificial, and I would have to agree, but now and then you have to be self-effacing and sacrificial, and considering the alternative (not seeing your grandchildren) I, for one, will willingly subdue my ire. On the other hand, there is a way of averting ever having to swallow hard. Abdicate the lead to your children with phrases like, "How do you usually do this?" or "What's your preference?" or "What would be most helpful for you?" or "How would you suggest I go about this?", "How would you like me to do this?"

Ways to avoid family tensions

I know all this sounds like perfect happy families, but friction is bound to arise sometimes, and this conciliatory approach is the antidote. There are certain tactics that will help you navigate these choppy waters. Over the years, and by talking to many grandparents, I've found there are certain *modi operandi* that seem to succeed where other strategies fail. These tactics aren't guarantees for averting family schisms, but they are worth trying. No doubt you can add to the list from your own experience.

Don't let your pride get the better of you What does it matter if you decide not to stand on ceremony and just give way? This is the opposite of feeling you've lived a life and therefore know best. Yes, you have lived a life and that has given you the wisdom and restraint to know when to back down.

Don't nurse resentment It will show in your behaviour. You may try to hide it, but you'll appear cold, judgemental and aloof. Even if you say nothing, your children will detect your feelings and simply won't want you around.

Don't bear grudges I know your children are very dear to your heart so it's quite hard to forgive, forget and move on, but move on you must. Life's too short.

Don't precipitate a show-down It's unforgivable and your children will never forget it. In the scheme of things it's never worth it, even if you have the satisfaction of knowing you've had your say – some satisfaction if your children don't want to see you any more afterwards. Think long-term.

Don't take sides between parents Even if one of them is your child and you feel a natural affinity to them, and the other is your in-law, it's never wise to take sides. Your job is to be an ally to both, and your position is on the middle ground. Otherwise you're bound to upset one of them and you become a bone of contention – not a nice thing to be – and create a situation that may reverberate for years.

Avoid a Mexican stand-off What's to be gained by standing on your dignity? Only a reputation for being a recalcitrant, old stickler, that's what. And what's to be lost? Something much more important – a lot of joyful times with your grandchildren.

Differences of opinion

There are countless questions to which you and your children will come up with somewhat different answers. Some of these answers may arise from modern childrearing fashions and fads, which seem outlandish to you. Others may be the result of new research and changed thinking and practice with which you're unfamiliar. New government guidelines on childhood vaccinations may seem unduly onerous on your baby grandchild, but it's not helpful to say so because your grandchild is going to be given them anyway, and voicing opposition will only make your child insecure. Your child or child-in-law may have read a book on bringing up babies and swallowed the theory hook, line and sinker. You may disagree with some or all of it, but it would be unwise to air your views because doing so would undermine your child's confidence and be tantamount to your saying you think he or she is a bad parent.

All sorts of practices have changed since you were bringing up babies, many of them with good reason, so it would be wise to bone up on any contentious issues before airing your point of view. Read the latest babycare book, go on to the sort of website that deals with childhood vaccinations. Read all you can on MMR, get a copy of the book your child seems hooked on and read it. You'll only be doing what you wished your own mother had done when your childrearing views clashed. And you'll have done very well indeed if you practise what you preached to your own mother when you said, "I'll bring up my children the way I want to without any interference from you".

Childcare issues

Judging from my postbag, these are some of the most common matters for disagreement between parents and grandparents.

Weaning In the old days mixed feeding could be introduced from four months onwards, but now World Health Organization guidelines admonish mothers who do so before six months. Most experts agree that a baby does best if its sole source of food is breast milk for six months, though bottlefed babies will nonetheless thrive. It's tempting, I know, to want to embark on mixed feeding if a baby seems to be hungry all the time or isn't sleeping through the night, but early mixed feeding isn't the answer. We now know so much about the connection between introducing mixed feeding too soon and allergies that we tend to hold back.

a baby does best if his sole source of food is **breast milk** *for six months*

Respecting each other's views

Depending on how strongly your children feel about an issue, there's always room for low-key, sensible discussion in which each of you is prepared to understand the other's point of view and, if necessary, learn from it. An example for me was when one of my daughters-in-law, a believer in complementary medicine, wanted to forgo my grandchild's MMR and opt for a herbal alternative that claimed to provide equivalent protection. Having read most of the research on MMR, and written on its safety, and knowing there was no herbal equivalent, my heart quaked. Where was the middle ground?

I asked my highly intelligent and eminently sensible daughter-in-law if she had any literature on the herbal equivalent. She had, and she passed it on to me. She, for her part, asked if I could give her a pack of my articles, so we read each other's pet theories. She confessed that she felt beleaguered by the advocates of both sides of the argument and felt resistant to being browbeaten by anyone (including me?). Even though I have been a protagonist of MMR since it became available and I've read nothing to change my mind, I didn't try to press my point of view on my daughter-in-law. I felt what she needed most was time and space to make up her own mind rather than my backing her up against a wall.

Three weeks later she told me that my grandchild had had the MMR. She said, on balance, she was too scared not to give it. And there are worse reasons for decisions than that.

79

I also remember introducing my own babies to animal protein – meat, chicken, fish, eggs and cheese – quite early on. You may remember the same, but the practice is outdated. The accepted paradigm these days is baby rice as a first step, graduating to one additional fruit or one additional vegetable at, say, weekly intervals. Rich animal protein is eschewed by most parents now until their baby is nine, ten or eleven months, perhaps even a year. Our babies are taller and healthier than ever before, and their life expectancy is approaching 120, so who's to say modern parents are wrong? Not I.

Our babies are **taller and healthier** *than ever before...so who's to say modern parents are wrong?*

Crying   I was someone who never let my babies cry on the grounds that I wanted them to grow up believing if they asked for attention, someone heard and went to them. My mother was of an even older school whose philosophy subscribed to the belief that it exercised a baby's lungs to cry for half an hour, and that they came to no harm if they cried unheeded for that long. I could never have done this; my nerves couldn't have borne it. Of course my way of doing things was hard on both my husband and myself, as we did duty on alternate nights and our two youngest sons were wakeful babies.

My children and stepchildren aren't unkind parents, but they opted for a modern method of handling a baby's crying, especially when put

Miriam's mailbag

Q Is my granddaughter getting cold?
My daughter had a lovely little girl on Christmas Day and we are so proud. My worry is that I don't think my daughter is wrapping her up enough. She has loose covers on her and her hands and cheeks are always cold. She says the baby mustn't get hot, but this is winter and when the heating isn't on, the house is cold. The baby cries a lot and I don't know if it's wind or if she's cold. I'm frightened to interfere. My daughter does everything by the baby book, even as far as not putting a little bit of talc on her when she's had a bath.

a Let your daughter do things her way
I think your daughter is right on both counts: no talc on baby skin, ever, it irritates it; and keeping the baby cool rather than hot. We've learned to our cost that keeping a baby on the warm side is a factor in causing *sudden infant death* (SIDS). This is because a baby can't regulate its temperature down when overheated – hence the heat rash so common in babies. Babies lose heat from the front of their chests, face, head and hands, so all of these should be left uncovered, and a baby should lie on its back to allow heat loss.

You're right not to interfere, though I know it's hard. Keep your own counsel and let your daughter bring up her baby the way she thinks best.

down at night to sleep, which I suppose is a hybrid of what I and my mother did. When I was first introduced to this method I found it heartbreakingly difficult to comply with, but it never occurred to me to flout their wishes. Their approach involves three principles, which go something like this:

- Every baby has the right to enjoy her cot and sleeping in it, but she can't enjoy it if she cries unheeded for long periods.
- With her parents' help, every baby can eventually learn to quieten herself.
- A parent's or carer's (this could be a grandparent) presence is initially necessary to soothe crying.

The method my son wanted me to follow (which I did to the letter) was to put his baby down, and if she was crying after five minutes, go to her cot and wordlessly stroke her or pat her, then leave the room. After five more minutes, repeat this little ritual, and so on until she stopped crying. On the first evening she cried for 40 agonizing minutes, on the second for 30 minutes, on the third for 15 minutes and on the fourth and thereafter not at all. Well now, had I learned a lesson? How I wish my son could have taught me this earlier and I'd have been saved countless interrupted nights.

Bedtimes I was a full-time working mum and wanted to see my children when I got home from work, so I was very relaxed about bedtimes. It seemed to me that my children went to sleep at approximately the same time whether I put them to bed and they larked about for an hour and a half till sleep overtook them, or they frolicked around me and fell asleep at my side on a sofa as I was reading, or at my feet when I was working at the kitchen table. I then scooped them up and put them down happily in their cot or bed.

Miriam's mailbag

Q **Is my mother-in-law right – are dummies harmful?**
My mother-in-law disapproves of dummies and is always making snide remarks about my three-year-old who still likes his dummy now and then. I take no notice as it's none of her business anyway. I can bring up my kids as I like. But she's put a doubt in my mind and I can't get rid of it. Could a dummy do my little boy harm?

a **Dummies can have benefits!**
Shame on your mother-in-law. She should know better and bite her tongue. Of course you have the right to raise your children as you think fit. Modern dummies are safe and don't harm babies in any way. They're a very effective source of comfort. And I thought you might like to know a benefit of dummies that I've picked up for you.

Some new research has shown that using a dummy at bedtime and during sleeping seems to reduce the risk of cot death (SIDS). The researchers seem to think a dummy can lower the risk factors of SIDS – to suck a dummy a baby has to lie on its back, which is the safest position for avoiding cot death. I wonder how your mother-in-law will react to this news?

Modern dummies are safe

The present generation of parents would view my domestic arrangements with horror. They, quite reasonably, want evenings to themselves. They want downtime and me time. I'm all in favour of this, but it involves a much tighter bedtime ritual than mine – bath, books, bottle and bed by 7pm. And I comply. I do miss long, joyful baths, lots of stories and gentle games, long goodnights with cuddles and songs. But my children know best and I've learned from them yet again.

I didn't know until they demonstrated it to me that *the more a child sleeps, the more a child sleeps.* So a sound nap in the afternoon doesn't mean a later bedtime, and an early bedtime doesn't mean an earlier wakening. A baby put to bed at 7pm will sleep a full 12 hours or more. A child having less sleep, say going to bed at 8:30, is more likely to have interrupted nights and early wakening.

My children *know best*
and I've learned from them yet again

Discipline I hate the word, but there doesn't seem to be an alternative. I don't believe in disciplining children – my mother did, with a very firm hand. I believe in encouraging and rewarding children from the outset. This is clearly dodgy ground if you and your child don't see eye to eye, and if they turn out to be more authoritarian than you, it will cause you pain. If, on the other hand, they're more lax, you could get very uptight and wound up.

By and large, present-day parents seem to manage discipline much better than my generation. They seem to be firm in the situations that warrant firmness and otherwise very laid-back and relaxed. They seem to understand, as I never did, that it's possible to bring up children, certainly for the first two years, without ever raising their voices. And the results are there for all to see. The most secure child I've ever come across is one of my granddaughters, who has only heard loving words since the day she was born from both her mother and her father. Even when disaster strikes they still smile and make light of it ("Never let her see you frightened, shocked and frowning," I remember my daughter-in-law wisely saying.) So this child is comfortable with strangers and new situations, she's smiley and outgoing, she separates from her parents without a scene, she takes adversity in her stride, she never cries for long, she'll let anyone put her to bed and she goes down happily.

In this scenario it would be a brave grandparent indeed who suggested things might be done differently, even though not everything conforms to how I think it might be done.

If you were to find that your child believed in the reverse – for example, in punitive methods or even in beating your grandchild – I'd still advocate not precipitating a showdown. This might mean your not being around to comfort your grandchild and act as a much-needed antidote to an aggressive parent.

By and large, present-day parents seem to manage discipline much better than my generation

Miriam's mailbag

Q How can I stop my mother-in-law monopolizing my daughter?

I had a reasonable relationship with my mother-in-law until my daughter was born last year. She wanted to be present during the delivery, but I really didn't want anyone but my husband there and she was really annoyed with me. When I went into labour my husband called her and she turned up at the hospital, but the midwife made her stay outside. She got annoyed with me again when I refused to let her take my baby back to her house for the afternoon when she was only a few days old. I know my daughter is very special to her because she's fallen out with her other son and he doesn't allow her to see his three children. But I hate the way she's always angling to monopolize my daughter. She wants to take her to her house every day, which is too much. And she's the type who believes in the spare the rod, spoil the child philosophy, which is abhorrent to me. What should I do?

a Nip this problem in the bud – now

If you have opposing ideas about raising children I can see why you're worried that your daughter may pick up mixed messages about discipline and even one day find herself on the receiving end of a smack from her grandmother. I'm sure your mother-in-law would never

deliberately wish any harm to her grandchild, but your daughter could be damaged by having two people around her with different ideas of what's right and what's wrong. And if your mother-in-law is the domineering and controlling type there are bound to be clashes ahead if you don't nip this in the bud now.

Bonding with her grandchild may be important to her, but your rights as the baby's mother mustn't be pushed to one side in the process. As a new mum you don't need someone constantly breathing down your neck and making you feel squeezed out. She may think she means well, giving you time to yourself, but she could be hogging your daughter to fill a void in her own life. What you must do is to say that your mother-in-law must come to your home to see the baby. This way she'll still have the fun of playing with her granddaughter, but she won't be usurping your position, and you can have direct control of any discipline issues. I hope you can count on your husband to side with you, for the sake of his daughter if nothing else. If he's too cowardly, be strong and put your foot down. You know it makes sense.

But *your rights* as the baby's mother mustn't be pushed to one side in the process

Eating Just as I thought there was nothing magical about sleeping in beds, I didn't think it was essential to eat at the table. It's a difficult task for a lively toddler to sit still and be orderly about eating. Trying to enforce order can be dispiriting for both of you. You can't force your child to eat, and you set up both you and your child for failure.

The way toddlers grow and develop means they actually can't physically conform to mealtimes. Unlike a baby in the first year, who's growing so fast that she'll gorge on regular meals three or four times a day, a toddler is growing more slowly and in spurts. So a toddler's appetite is unpredictable. Toddlers are designed to graze anywhere and any time, not just at the table. You'll get more food into them with this informal approach than you ever will with strict regimes.

Most parents these days are prepared to do whatever it takes to make sure their child eats well in terms of what they consume in a day, irrespective of when and where they eat it. I know from my postbag that grandparents are often disapproving of this approach, which they see as haphazard and not encouraging good habits and proper table manners. If you fall into this camp, I'd be subtle about raising the subject with your child. You're present for a few meals at most. They manage their child's eating day in and day out and have arrived at a routine that works for them. Who's to say it could be improved upon with more formality? No child is harmed by happy eating. No child will eat if they're unhappy. You choose.

Keep a *relaxed* approach
to eating and *mealtimes*

Miriam's mailbag

Q Isn't my daughter-in-law being unfair?

I adore my three-year-old grandson. We're very close and have lots of fun together playing in the park and feeding the ducks. The problem is that his mother, my daughter-in-law, sometimes interferes with our relationship. She tells me what he can and can't do, including what he eats. She objects when I give him anything sweet. Sometimes I tell him not to tell his mum when we've had a few sweeties. Now she's found out about our little secret, and is threatening to stop me seeing him because she says she can't trust me.

a You've broken her trust

You have broken her trust so you've only got yourself to blame. It doesn't matter if you have differing ideas about what's good and bad for your grandson. She's his mum and all the authority lies with her.

You've been very unfair to your grandson too, giving him conflicting messages about sweets. You've encouraged him to be disloyal and to lie to his mum. What can help? To begin with, beg and plead for your daughter-in-law's forgiveness and promise never to be sneaky again. And in future, steer clear of activities that could create conflict. It's one thing to remember what it was like to be a child, quite another to make the mistake of acting like one!

You can't spoil a child with love.
That isn't spoiling – it's *loving*

Spoiling Everyone has a different definition of what constitutes spoiling, but we all know it when we see it. It amounts to a child's every demand being given in to. And as each demand is met, successive demands escalate into the realms of indulgence. A child who has been spoiled this way will resort to tears and tantrums if their demands are not met, and the ritual having become established, a parent will give in to their child once again.

You can't, however, spoil a child with love. That isn't spoiling – it's loving, and it has exactly the opposite effect to the kind of spoiling described above. The loved child is generous, loving, affectionate and prepared to share, as opposed to the spoiled child who is unfriendly, insecure, scowling, cold, unloving, demanding, and won't share things on any account.

Grandparents can sometimes find themselves crossing the line from loving to spoiling. If your children are staunch believers in not spoiling, you run a serious risk of falling out with them, especially if you try to keep it secret and spoil your grandchild behind their backs. You have to see your actions for what they are. You're trying to curry favour, to buy love and affection from your grandchildren with forbidden treats. There's nothing more calculated to upset your children.

I've been guilty of being less firm over certain things than my children wish me to be. They've said to me that I "give in" to my grandchildren and sometimes I do. I can't help it. And sometimes when my children are present I plead with them to give in too. I remember one occasion when my grandchild wanted something very much and her parents denied her. She started to cry and still she was denied. I, meantime, was getting more and more agitated. Then she played her trump card " PLEASE may I have...". "Oh," I said, "Do let her have it as she's saying please" (a hard word to get out of her at the time). "No", came the flat reply, and I hung my head silently.

Health While you may disagree with your children about the approach to one of their own or your grandchildren's health problems, I don't think you should hang back about expressing your view if the problem is serious. Indeed, I'd go further and say you might follow the tack of positive intervention. You would have a lot of constructive things to say and do if, for instance, a grandchild was anorexic, or was self-harming or on drugs. Health questions of this magnitude are family problems and are better dealt with if they're shared, as long as your input is positive and supportive. As someone with a lifetime's experience, you're probably the one who would advocate involving your grandchildren in all the health decisions that affect them, and would be the first to take a constructive approach by asking questions rather than taking an authoritarian line. Questions such as:

"How can we help you?"

"What would you like us to do?"

"What makes you want to harm yourself/reject food/take drugs?"

"Who would you like to help you?"

You might also find yourself as the arbitrator between grandchild and parent, and personally I would support whichever one of them most needs your help. You won't go far wrong in any family dispute if you put the child (your grandchild) first.

Miriam's mailbag

Q How should my son tackle my granddaughter's bad behaviour?

My 14-year-old granddaughter lives with my son and is making his life a misery. She has lived with him for the past five years and now doesn't have contact with her mum, which is of her own choosing. She's naughty, lies, and runs up massive phone bills. Her bedroom is like a pigsty and she's been in trouble at school. My son has tried to give her everything she needs, but she throws it back in his face and obviously thinks he's failed as a parent. His fiancée is at her wits' end and my son is sure his daughter will split them up. She seems to be very jealous of his fiancée and does her best to upset her, although so far she hasn't succeeded. I've been telling my son he should lay down the law and ground her – don't you agree?

a She needs support, not criticism

Well no, I don't, and welcome to the world of a typical teenager! Parents all over the country will be sympathizing with your son as they're wading knee-deep through discarded clothes and other assorted mess left by their teens. But hassling her about her room is unlikely to reap any dividends. It's best for dad to close the door and ignore it.

He's unlikely to persuade her to become a domestic princess, but if he asks for her suggestions on how they can work together to keep the family rooms reasonably tidy she

might cooperate. Start with small things that are easy to do and don't expect miracles. We can never give a child enough praise, and I suspect she, more than most, needs the reassurance that she's loved and wanted. A teen who's given the message they're lazy with no self-control is likely to respond negatively. Pay more attention to good behaviour than bad. No matter how atrocious a parent might be, it takes a lot for a child to close the door on them. Even if she'll never admit it, your granddaughter must miss having two parents in her life and all this troublesome behaviour is symptomatic of someone who's hurting. She is, after all, still a child, with all the limitations and lack of experience that implies.

Can you blame her for being jealous of her prospective stepmum if she's desperate to be in the centre of her dad's world? It's bad enough going through the trials and tribulations of adolescence without feeling completely out on a limb. He may give her everything she wants materially, but how much undivided attention does she get? Building up shared interests with her, even if it's just watching some of her favourite soaps together, may help. Contacting the Parentline Plus helpline on 0808 800 2222, which offers support to anyone parenting a child, is something else to consider.

Don't lose faith in her. She may not be perfect but she needs to know you're on her side. And instead of encouraging your son to read the riot act, you could play a very important supportive role to help your granddaughter cope with her very deep unhappiness. You could try meeting up for a chat and a meal – and give your granddaughter a lot of love.

Multiple sets of grandparents

I know how it feels to be one of several sets of grandparents, and as second and third marriages are quite common these days it's an increasingly frequent phenomenon. If both sets of parents of the couple are alive there will be at least two sets of grandparents, and if a couple turns to one set rather than another, sees or visits them more frequently or is in closer proximity to one set than the other, it's easy to understand how jealousies and rivalries come about.

It could be that one set is better off than the other and can afford more financial support in the form of helping with house purchase, holidays, school fees, a new car. Then the other grandparents may feel like the poor relatives if they want to see themselves in that light. Another way of looking at it, however, is to be happy that your children have such generous benefactors who can give them a standard of living they and your grandchildren wouldn't otherwise enjoy. You in your turn can give your grandchildren gifts which mean just as much, if not more: time, interest, outings that cost little but are enormous fun, love, focused attention, and simple games that you regularly participate in.

Avoid rivalries It would be a pity to let rivalries come between you and your children and grandchildren. In any event your children won't have the same point of view and will wonder what you find so upsetting, or simply lose patience with you.

In my own extended family, one set of grandparents lives in America and sees their child and grandchild rarely and fleetingly. They are exemplary. There's absolutely no rivalry between them and us – quite the opposite. They're grateful that we can help their child and we're there for her family whenever they're in need.

Miriam's mailbag

Q My daughter's always with her in-laws

They say a son is a son until he gets him a wife and a daughter is a daughter for all of her life. That's not true in our case. My daughter got married last year and has a baby girl, but now her whole life seems to revolve around her new husband and his family. It's like her father and I don't exist any more and it really hurts. When she does bother to phone, she only talks about what she's been doing with the other grandparents. I've been so looking forward to being a grandma. I've complained, and she accused me of being jealous!

a Show an interest

Admit it. You are jealous. You feel cast aside when really you should be feeling proud as punch that you've raised a daughter more than capable of getting along with the family she's married into. For some people, getting on with the in-laws is a lifelong challenge, but she seems to have it sussed already. Show an interest. This is all new to her, so let her know you care she's been accepted by them. How about moving along with your own life and finding some new and interesting things to do that you can tell her about?

*admit it – you're **jealous***

Miriam's mailbag

Q **Am I right to feel not wanted?**
My daughter-in-law is 25 and the youngest of six children. Her family get together to celebrate every conceivable occasion. Her family is at our son's house all the time and we are hardly ever invited. We wouldn't dream of just turning up without an invitation. My son's an only child, as were my husband and myself, so we've no living relatives. I feel very left out, resentful and upset. Am I right to feel not wanted?

a **Don't stand on ceremony – get in touch**
Your in-laws seem to be spontaneous people who can arrange a knees-up at the drop of a hat, while by nature, you're more aloof.

You could be your own worst enemy if you always feel a formal invitation is required to visit your family. I doubt the intention's to deliberately exclude you, but they may need affirmation you're a bit of a party animal on the quiet. While it's good you respect other people's boundaries, if you lighten up and don't always stand on ceremony, you might find yourself where you really want to be – in the middle and not stuck out on the edge. Don't just turn up, but phone and ask if you can babysit, take the baby out for a walk or just have a chat.

phone and offer to babysit

Blood relationships count   With multiple step-parent and step-grandparent combinations I think it's wise to recognize that the blood relationship counts more and should take precedence. Anything else would be bizarre. You're a wise grandparent if you place your trust in your grandchildren. If you're a good, loving grandparent they'll nose you out and ask for you. Later on when they're old enough, they'll vote with their feet and come and visit you.

Overload

For the past 10 years I've been receiving letters from grandparents who are providing childcare for their children in order to allow them to work, sometimes full-time, and enjoy a higher standard of living. Many grandparents in this situation find it difficult to meet the expectations of their children.

- In the first place, many are of an age where strength and stamina are finite and they find full-time childcare utterly exhausting.
- Most grandparents, while wanting to help their children out, didn't expect their retirement to consist of working many hours a day as a

Newsflash

At the time of writing there are 13.5 million grandparents in the UK, and statistics show that they provide about 60 per cent of childcare in this country. More than 90 per cent of first-time mothers get grandma to help with the baby. Government figures show that childcare provided by grandparents saves the economy up to £4 billion a year.

glorified childminder, and much as they adore their grandchildren, they often feel taken for granted.

● This feeling is made even worse when the children think mum's a soft touch, she'll do it out of love, and they don't or won't pay for a grandparent's help.

Most grandparents aren't concerned about money per se, but the lack of acknowledgement for their efforts is extremely hurtful and they can see no way out – they don't want to be a financial burden for their children, but nor do they wish to suffer themselves.

Couples should beware of asking parents to do too much, or there could be a big falling-out. Grandparents would be wise to be very clear and firm about what they're prepared to do and not do, and the basis for any payment should be fairly agreed.

*Couples should **beware** of asking grandparents to do too much, or there could be a big falling-out*

Favouritism

I'd be the first to concede that it isn't always easy to be scrupulously fair with your attention, even though you make a concerted effort to do so. And it's especially hard when you're pulling out the stops to treat all your children and grandchildren equally, and another grandparent defies the rules of fairness and openly dotes on the child

Miriam's mailbag

Q My mother-in-law favours my son

My mother-in-law often shows favouritism towards my son, aged five, at the expense of our youngest child, a daughter aged two. She's always commenting on the clever things he's said or done, but she rarely says anything nice about our daughter. I know our daughter is very young, but I feel she already notices that her brother get more attention from grandma than she does. I love both my children equally and I'm upset on her behalf.

a You're right to be concerned

You're right to be uneasy, because all children should think they're fabulous and wonderful to be around, especially in families. Perhaps because he's the firstborn your son can do no wrong, or maybe your mother-in-law has a hard time relating to girls? Whatever the reason, grandma needs to start acting like a grown-up and stop treating her granddaughter as second best. She's missing out on a really special little girl and your daughter is being unfairly sidelined.

Ultimately, as parents, you're responsible for protecting your daughter from this kind of emotional neglect and it's vital you express your concerns about the favouritism. If she won't listen, you'd be justified in limiting or restricting her contact with the children.

Miriam's mailbag

Q The shock of my life!

I've just had the shock of my life! My daughter-in-law has confessed to me that my oldest granddaughter isn't my son's biological child. She's made me promise to keep her secret and I've agreed. They have two beautiful girls aged 14 and 11. I love both girls with all my heart and I'm especially close to the eldest. I don't know what to think.

a She's still your granddaughter

It's no wonder you're in shock. Your daughter-in-law has been keeping a mighty big secret and she must have a lot of faith in you to trust you with the truth. This type of family secret isn't rare. You would be surprised to know how many people are, like your granddaughter, not the offspring of the man who raised them. This news doesn't have to destroy your relationship with your grandchild. Already your special bond transcends any blood tie. She'll still be your granddaughter and your love for her won't change, unless that's what you want, which I'm sure you don't.

of a particular child. This can even happen between grandparents. Granny, on the one hand, strives to be even-handed with the grandchildren of her son and daughter. Grandpa, on the other, may make no bones about the fact that he dotes on his daughter's grandchildren, partly because they were his first grandchildren, partly because they're girls and being girls they spoil him rotten and are always well-behaved. This has the potential of causing much unhappiness in the family. Grandpa's son can find this intensely irritating and frustrating. He feels grandpa's favouritism doesn't reflect only on his children (three boys) but makes him somehow a second-class person too. He feels he can't live up to his father's expectations, and relations right across the family will be strained and tense till this wrong can be righted.

Mind you, it may never be righted, but recrimination will only open old wounds. It may be up to granny to persuade her son that the thing to do is not to dissipate emotional energy on being jealous of the attention given to his sister's children. Better to concentrate on his own family and reap the joyous harvest that he has sown with them.

Estrangement through divorce

Grandparents can find themselves the unwitting victims of a complicated marriage split, as the parents of the estranged ex with the loss of access to their grandchildren. Make no mistake, the parent who has care of your grandchildren has all the power, including the power to deny you access to your grandchildren.

Quite often, in an acrimonious divorce, the children's carer will do anything they can to hurt the ex's family, including you, irrespective of a painful parting of their children from their grandparents. Bitterness can fuel spiteful actions that are clearly not in your grandchild's interests. But you may not have the leverage to negotiate some kind of arrangement to see your grandchildren when the aggrieved party tars you with the same brush as their ex.

You can try appealing to the estranged parent of your grandchildren, but I receive many letters from grandparents who haven't seen their grandchildren for years and are at a loss to know what to do. You can keep open the channels of communication with letters, Christmas and birthday cards and presents, little notes to say hello, text messages, emails and photographs. Just wave every now and then and trust your grandchildren will know you're one of the good guys.

Money

There are few subjects that elicit stronger and more polarized views than money and, after a lifetime of hard work, saving and keeping a nest egg intact, it's hard to stand by a profligate child and their family.

You may be a generous grandparent who helps out financially as much as you can, and when you see money being frittered away you may long to remonstrate with your spendthrifts. But, as I've said elsewhere in this book, giving money to your children doesn't give you the right to say how it's spent. If you feel so strongly about how it's spent that you want to dictate the conditions of your loan/gift or question your child's judgement if their choices are different from yours, you always have the option of not giving it – perhaps better than precipitating a row.

You can always call a halt to future loans and gifts if your child isn't more responsible. But what do you do about your grandchildren? It isn't their fault that their parents can't hold on to money, and the

Miriam's mailbag

Q How can we persuade my in-laws to visit us?
We're a low-income family with only my husband's wages coming in and we have three children under the age of six. My husband's parents are both in their fifties and in good health, yet they expect us to drive for an hour with the children to visit them. It's not just the time involved. Quite often we simply don't have the money to put petrol in the car for the journey. How can we persuade them to make more effort to visit us for the children's sake?

a Tell them the truth
Your in-laws are being very thoughtless. It only takes minimal effort for them to get in their car and make the journey, whereas for you it's a military operation to load the little ones in the car and keep them amused. It's time they woke up to the reality that your time and money are both under pressure. Why don't you and your husband write them a nice letter explaining the situation? Be honest about the obstacles that make it difficult for you to do all the visiting. Don't be embarrassed to explain to them about how you sometimes struggle to make ends meet and emphasize how much you're looking forward to seeing them at your home.

last thing you'd want is for them to suffer. You may find yourself so pained by this thought that you continue supporting your child against your better judgement.

Conversely you may find that your children are so independent and such good managers that you have to tread warily when making an offer of financial help. In this instance, I try to get round it by saying it's a loan and I can be paid back when they're out of the woods.

No-go areas

If you're the same generation as me you may remember that mind-numbing bigot Alf Garnett, in the television programme *Till Death Us Do Part*. Alf's son-in-law handled him beautifully, with disparaging wit, cutting humour and unfailing good nature. If you can't be as resilient, you could come a cropper if you take on bigotry, prejudice and bias in your children and in-laws in whatever arena.

Religion   Even within families tempers can flare on the subject of religion, and threatening rifts open up. I was raised in an orthodox Jewish family, but I left Judaism at the age of 14. For a child of orthodox parents there is no greater sin than to "marry out" – to marry a non-Jew. I married a Quaker. My father had no option, according to his religion, but to shred his clothing as an act of grief and bereavement, remove all traces of me from the family home, close up my bedroom and declare I was dead. There was no place for compromise in this situation, and despite my weekly telephone calls asking for a rapprochement, my father failed even to acknowledge that I was alive for two years. It took a further year for him to admit that I was his daughter.

I tell this story not to recriminate but to illustrate that with fundamentalist religious fervour there is often no room for negotiation. And in a case of religious mixed marriage there is little chance that the overture will be accepted. My husband, my father's son-in-law, didn't exist either as far as my father was concerned and this dissonance put enormous strain on the marriage. Thank heavens there weren't any children from that marriage. My father's behaviour to me seemed bizarre and eccentric enough, but had it been directed towards my children I'd have found it unforgivable.

I discuss my own case only as an example. I get many letters from inter-religious couples who can do nothing to persuade their parents to accept and welcome their spouse. As a parent I can't imagine remaining in a religion that demanded I desert my children or reject their chosen partner, but religious beliefs die hard and are often immovable.

Even within families tempers flare on the subject of **religion,** *and threatening rifts can open up*

Race   As a little girl I remember my father often saying that he regarded the black man as his brother but he didn't want him to marry one of his daughters. My father was a deeply religious man, but any arguments against his racist stance met with deaf ears. It was impossible to talk to him on the subject of intermarriage of any kind; he would angrily bring any conversation on the subject to an abrupt halt.

My mother was quite different. I remember her telling me of a dance she'd gone to as a young woman, and a black man was standing at the side of the dance floor looking on. Each time he asked a white girl to dance he was refused. My mother, affronted by this behaviour, marched up to him and asked him to dance. He turned out to be very good, and they danced the rest of the evening together. My mother was concerned only about his way with a quickstep, not the colour of his skin.

Later, my parents were tested when my younger sister married an African-American, and all the old chestnuts about the difficulties, real and potential, of interracial marriages were aired. None of them mattered, none of them were useful and none of them were helpful. My sister hoed her own row and made a magnificent job of it.

Nowadays one of the most common problems I'm faced with in my postbag is that of the Muslim/Christian couple. It seems that parents on neither side will support their children in what is their child's decision. On this and many other vexed questions, children have the right to lead their own lives. Our role as parents is only to support them and, I strongly believe, be there for them if things should go wrong. To do anything else is fruitless. Your child or grandchild will do as they wish whatever you say, and you'll end up making an enemy of yourself. In five years' time when you look back, is that how you wish to be remembered?

A grandparent's role is to **support** *children and grandchildren and* **be there** *if things go wrong*

Politics Feelings run just as high over politics as they do over religion and race. Our political persuasion says so much about ourselves, and many people for one reason or another are unswerving in their political beliefs, sometimes against all reason. I remember a story about my grandfather told to me by a great-uncle. My grandfather was a miner working in the Durham coalfields and was one of the Jarrow marchers He was a devoted trade union man and put his trade union above all else, even his family. He's reported to have said, "It's easy to stand by the trade union when you know them to be right, but it's hard when you know them to be wrong".

Such strongly held political views brook no questioning and risk a dangerous conflict of wills and beliefs if tackled head-on. Hot-headed political rows can tear a family apart, whether between generations or across generations. I've always allowed discretion to be the better part of valour and skirted around political topics. Confrontations never fail to leave bruises, if not open wounds, which can take years to heal. Keeping your own counsel is a wise strategy.

Education Every parent wants the best education they can afford for their children, and with our hypocritical socialist leaders preaching state education for all but sending their children to private schools, no parent can be blamed for opting to do the same thing. However, you may be a great believer in state education and be affronted if your children opt to bypass it when it comes to your grandchildren. The opposite may equally apply, where you worry for a grandchild in the state system and feel their personalities or special needs may be better served by a private education. You may even feel like offering to pay for it. If your child staunchly believes in comprehensive schooling that would only add insult to injury, so you may choose to stay out of the argument.

Sex The sexual predilections of couples rarely match, so it would be too much to expect that your attitudes will chime with those of your children or grandchildren. With your grandchildren the generation gap can be as wide as the ocean, so it's very unlikely that you'll see eye to eye. Your children and grandchildren will expect you to have puritan views and belong to the "just say no" school, so you'd surprise them if you came up with something more enlightened and constructive. No one can stop anyone who wants to have sex from having it, but with a low-key, objective approach it's possible to steer a youngster in the direction of averting most of the mishaps.

If you're an open-minded, reasonable person you may find a grandchild comes to you with their sexual dilemma rather than face their parents, and you may be called upon to be a go-between. No one is better qualified for such a role and it's a great compliment if your grandchild turns to you for support. There's only one thing to do in this situation and that's give guidance, even though it may risk a confrontation with your child.

Clothes and appearance As fashions come and go in the blink of an eye, it would be an unusual grandparent who was in tune with what their grandchildren, or even their children, were wearing or, for that matter, what they highly prize. It can be hard to get into a teenage grandchild's mindset – the mindset that only one particular trainer or pair of jeans will do – and what seems to you a gross extravagance is to them as important as food; more important, in fact.

It helps if you can see beyond the clothes, the jewellery or the weird hairstyle. I remember my number three son stating defiantly that he wanted a punk hairdo. I told him there was nothing wrong with that and offered to get him an appointment with my hairdresser. He duly

Miriam's mailbag

Q Where are their values?

I'm 80 years old and I feel most people these days don't seem to have any values. I'm sad to admit my grandson, who's 24, is one of them. Although I've always had a particularly soft spot for him, I think he's let me and the rest of the family down by getting his girlfriend pregnant. Even now the baby's been born, there's still no hint of any wedding plans. I'm finding it very hard to accept that my grandson and his girlfriend don't mind their little daughter being illegitimate.

a Try to accept this new family member

All children are equally legitimate, and thankfully in Britain today illegitimacy no longer carries the strong social stigma it once did. I realize it's hard for you to accept that the typical family of your youth no longer exists, and that families now come in many different shapes and sizes, but this doesn't make them any less genuine. Surely the most important thing is your great-granddaughter is loved and wanted by both her parents, not that there's a wedding certificate tucked away in the back of a drawer? Please don't allow what this young couple have done, or not done, to come between you and the new member of the family.

went along, got his dyed blonde Mohican, and I paid for it. His father was appalled, but I wasn't about to fall out with my son over a haircut. What's more, I admired his chutzpah. The Mohican didn't last long.

To my mind, it's a cause for celebration that your children and grandchildren are so engaged, curious, and brave about life that they're prepared to experiment with clothes, hair, jewellery, even body piercing, and if you think of their eccentricities in this way, your criticism may freeze on your lips.

Friendships I don't think there's a parent or grandparent around who doesn't think that their children and grandchildren have the odd unsuitable friend. Friendship runs deep, and your child or grandchild will take it as a criticism of them if you disparage their friends. How much better a comment like, "Your friend seems so interesting. Do you think I could meet him and get to know him a bit better?"

Healing rifts

Here are some ways of healing rifts that have worked for me.

Eat humble pie Don't hesitate for a second to say sorry or take responsibility. You already know from a lifetime of experience that an apology invariably pours oil on troubled waters. Why not give that marvellous gift to the people you love most? You'll quickly become known and loved for your generosity of spirit. Extend this model of ready apology to your grandchildren and you teach them the difficult step of saying sorry. So leap at the chance to say sorry to your grandchildren. Or the chance to say, "Silly Granny, I made a mistake there". You'll be repaid.

Bite your tongue Don't let criticism or interference pass your lips. If you do, you'll wish with all your heart you'd stopped the words from slipping out when you see your children's crestfallen or angry faces. Why risk a falling-out for the sake of making a point?

Practise selective amnesia Forget all the things that make you twitchy and concentrate only on the things that are real blessings. It's a vital trick to cultivate. First, this allows you to move on from difficulties with good grace. Second, you'll feel proud of yourself for being so grown-up. And third, your children will see you as a fair, just and loving parent who doesn't, thank heavens, let things rankle.

Be the first to offer the olive branch I have always believed that one of the prices we pay for being older than our children is that we act as peacemakers. For all sorts of reasons our children find it hard to leap the gap and make a peace-offering. We find it hard too, no doubt, but because of our long perspective it costs us less than it does them. In fact, we have nothing to prove.

Turn a blind eye Don't see things that upset you. Just acknowledge them to yourself and mollify yourself with a thought like, "Oh, that's how we do it here". Learn rather than retaliate. Think to yourself, "Glad I noticed that before I put my foot in it/opened my mouth."

Be a conciliatory negotiator – not an adversarial one. Given how much you love your children and grandchildren, why would you want to come over as an adversary? Your role is to help find common ground through give and take, with you doing most of the giving and your children doing most of the taking. What's wrong with that?

5 Doing things with your grandchildren

You may be concerned that doing things with your grandchild may demand more agility and stamina than you feel you can muster – and they might – but one of the most enjoyable and important activities is just reading books.

My working principle is that no baby is too young to be introduced to books. In practical terms this means when a baby is about two months old and has mastered focusing. While attention span is short at this age, the *idea* of looking at pictures and handling paper thrills a baby, especially if you're wholly engaged in turning pages and pointing at pictures together. Just watch your grandchild having a great time with the rustly pages of a magazine.

Sharing a book

Reading is particularly nourishing for that special relationship between grandparents and grandchildren: you're cuddled up together with your grandchild held close on your knee; you have a common interest – the book; you can chat about each page, each turn of event, each picture; you can demonstrate novelty items, such as flaps to lift; you can watch your grandchild growing and developing; you can teach your grandchild endlessly with concepts, ideas, vocabulary. It's never-ending and you can share wonderful intimate moments together. And you can do all of this with any book.

Books about grandparents You might want to read some books that are actually about grandparents. Despite the fact that so many parents rely on grandparents for childcare, there are precious few books about grandparents around, but here are a few good ones.

For grandchildren over nine years old there's the magical "great-great-grandmother" of Princess Irene in George Macdonald's delightful novels, *The Princess and the Goblin* and *The Princess and Curdie.*

The grandparents in Roald Dahl's *The Witches* or Lucy M. Boston's *Green Knowe* series are the kind of grandparents we'd all like to emulate – firm but deeply caring. And Lawrence Anholt's *Seven for a Secret* exemplifies the joys of staying in touch with grandchildren through letter-writing, something most of us could do more of. The six-year-old heroine Ruby swaps notes with her "grampa" who lives in the countryside; Ruby lives in the town. Their relationship develops with tales from each other's lives, even exchanging secrets, so that they grow very close to each other through the vehicle of correspondence. The book raises a lot of issues in a positive way and Anholt even draws bereavement into a child's world when Ruby's grandpa dies. This delightful book is illustrated with a picture of grampa dying in bed, but it's not at all frightening.

Some of my favourites

Here are some more books to read to your grandchildren.

- *Nana's Garden* (2+) by Sophy Williams. Available second-hand.
  A boy plays with a ghostly girl in his grandmother's garden.

- *When Grandma Came* (2+) by Jill Paton Walsh. Available
  second-hand. A travelling grandma's love for her granddaughter.

- *A Busy Day For A Good Grandmother* (3+) by Margaret Mahy.
  Available second-hand. Mrs Oberon will stop at nothing to help her
  son's teething baby. Hilarious.

- *Grandmothers' Stories* (4+) retold by Burleigh Muten.
  Barefoot Books. Excellent fairy tales.

It's possible that death and bereavement are best handled with pictures rather than words, as in Harry Horse's classic *The Last Polar Bears*. The book also features an adventurous grandfather, this time journeying to the North Pole. On the journey he sends back letters to his grandchild in a kind of gentle, gradual parting. Bear in mind that if you play an important role in your grandchildren's lives, your passing will be hard. These books can prepare the way beautifully.

As your grandchildren get older you can share books in another way – you read them separately, then discuss them together. See the box below for some suggestions. There are a number of books that blur the boundary between adults' and children's reading. Lewis Carroll, I suppose, was the first writer to do this with his *Alice* books, then there are all Tolkien's and C.S Lewis's works and, of course, the *Harry Potter* books and Philip Pullman's *His Dark Materials* trilogy.

Books to talk about

Here are some books you might want to take a look at and enjoy talking about with your grandchildren:

- *Cyrano* by Geraldine McCaughrean, Oxford University Press.

- *The Boy In Striped Pyjamas* by John Boyne, David Fickling Books.

- *Doctors & Nurses* by Lucy Ellman, Bloomsbury.

- *Blue Shoes and Happiness* by Alexander McCall Smith, Pantheon/Polygon.

Out and about

With a very young baby it's simply not worth undertaking a very busy outing during which you will have to walk a great deal, carry heavy loads, or make lots of transport changes. Be easy on yourself. Try to take a friend or your partner with you if you can, so there's always an extra pair of hands and someone to help should you get into difficulties. Your baby grandchild can go with you anywhere as long as you're well enough prepared and have something in which to carry him, such as a sling, pram, or car seat. I well remember carrying my first grandchild, a little girl of only a few weeks, in a sling one midwinter. I would trudge the streets talking to her non-stop, dodging into shops to keep the two of us warm. Passers-by would look at this mumbling woman as though she were mad, but my granddaughter and I were doing a spot of bonding.

Once your grandchild is weaned you'll have to carry food, a feeding dish, plastic spoon, bib, cup with a spout, a supply of drinks, and something for her to nibble on, such as pieces of dry toast or rusks. You can feed her directly from a jar, but remember that whatever she doesn't finish out of a feeding jar must be thrown away afterwards, because it will be contaminated with saliva, and germs will grow in it very quickly.

*Your baby grandchild can go with you **anywhere** as long as you're well enough prepared*

Remember – *the easiest time to be out and about with a baby is while she's* small and portable

Changing Even if your grandchild normally wears fabric nappies, forget the expense and take disposables with you on a journey. They're convenient for both you and your grandchild. You can always do the changing on the back seat of the car or in the boot if she lies on a rug or a towel. There's no need to do any more than top and tail while travelling. Wipes are essential, as is a nappy-sac for dirty nappies.

Going further afield The first few outings that involve more than pushing the pram round the local shops may seem daunting, and even though you're an old hand, you'll probably be a bit nervous and unsure about how your grandchild will react. Try to relax – she'll pick up on any anxieties you have. You'll soon become a family of seasoned travellers, and remember – the easiest time to be out and about with a baby is while she's small and portable. Make the most of it because when she's toddling and needing constant supervision, the range of outings will become more limited for a while and, as I've found out, much more tiring. Don't be too ambitious on your first outings – go to your local park, perhaps, or stop off for coffee in a café. Make sure you're confident about being away from home with your grandchild before you opt for something further afield. When you do, travel at off-peak times when there's less congestion, especially if you're going by bus or train.

The baby bag – never leave home without it!

Young baby

You'll need basic changing and feeding equipment and a toy:

- Changing bag or mat
- Disposable nappies
- Baby wipes
- Nappy cream
- Plastic bags for dirty nappies
- A bottle containing a whole feed if she's bottle-feeding
- Hat and cardigan
- A couple of favourite toys

Older baby

You'll need solid food, and feeding and changing equipment:

- Changing mat
- Fabric or disposable nappies
- Baby wipes
- Nappy cream
- Plastic bags for dirty nappies
- Baby food, dish, spoon
- Bib for feeding
- Snacks such as fruit
- Diluted fruit juice
- Sun hat or woollen hat
- Cardigan or sweater
- Comforter
- Favourite books and toys

Using a modern pushchair A pushchair is ideal for a baby from newborn, when he'll fit comfortably and snugly into its shape, up until two or three years old. Babies are interested in their surroundings from an early age, so as soon as your grandchild can sit up, angle the pushchair so that he can see what's going on around him. Recent research says that babies who face you probably talk earlier, so your family might like to consider this when investing in a pushchair.

You need to be adept at collapsing and opening the pushchair within a few seconds without any problems, so practise at home before your first outing. Just the other day I had to figure out how to get my

Pushchair safety tips

- When you open your pushchair, always make sure that it's in the fully extended position with the brakes **fully locked**.
- Never put your grandchild in a pushchair without a safety harness.
- **Never** ever leave her in a pushchair unattended.
- If she falls asleep in the pushchair, adjust it to the lie-back position so that she can sleep comfortably.
- Don't put shopping on the handles of the pushchair; it can unbalance the pushchair and your grandchild could be injured.
- When you stop, always put the **brakes on** because you could inadvertently take your hands off the pushchair and allow it to run away from you.
- Make sure the brakes and catches **work well** and that the wheels are solid.

Travelling on your own with a grandchild needs the **organization** *of a military operation*

granddaughter's pushchair to unfold with no one to refer to. I forget each time. Get instructions before you find yourself alone. If you can't fold up the pushchair efficiently, you'll find people jostling to get in front of you when you're in a queue, which will only add to your frustration. At the very least, you should be able to open it with one hand, kick it shut with your feet, and know how to operate the brakes. Don't forget you'll have to do all these things while holding the baby.

Using public transport If you're travelling with your children and grandchildren, you'll be a welcome extra pair of hands and eyes as long as you're weightless yourself. Travelling on your own with a grandchild needs the organization of a military operation.

Using public transport can be a challenge. Picture yourself with a pushchair, a heavy wriggling baby, the baby bag, your handbag and a coat, and public transport could be the last thing you want to face. It's as well to have grandpa or a friend with you for the really heavy and complicated journeys. Of course you can make things easier by never travelling in the rush hour or, if you have a very young grandchild, by carrying him around in a sling. For an older baby, a backpack can make you much more independent, and you can manage everything more easily with your hands free.

Transport tips

Planning ahead is the secret to trouble-free travel with babies and children by any form of public transport:

- If you're travelling alone, make sure you can manage everything yourself – although you may hope for offers of help, people aren't always as thoughtful to grandparents with babies as you may wish.
- Allow plenty of time to reach the station or airport to avoid the extra stress of worrying about missing a train or aeroplane.
- If you're flying long-haul, try to book a seat with a bassinet so that the baby can sleep during the flight.
- A portable car seat is invaluable, though for air travel you may have to pay for an extra seat on busy flights if you want to use one just for the baby.

Always prepare yourself well ahead of time. I never leave home with my grandchildren without some distracting toys, favourite books, drinks and favourite snacks. All your belongings, including the pushchair, should be collected together prior to leaving and in good enough time so that you can check them over to make sure that you haven't forgotten anything. The same goes for when you're getting off a bus or train; be ready to get off in plenty of time for your stop. Don't be shy – always ask for help from fellow-passengers.

Outings with grandchildren

No baby is ever too young for an outing; indeed, with a young baby you can go just about anywhere and, provided he can look about him, he will enjoy the change of scene, even if he doesn't understand quite what's going on.

When planning an outing for an older child, always try to consider what your grandchild's personality can cope with best. If he's a quiet child who has a long concentration span, you can take him to a flower show or an antique market and point out the things around him. If, on the other hand, he's very active, he'll need more space to run around in and plenty of things to do: a trip to the zoo, a playground or a fair may be more appropriate.

Baby-friendly activities

There are plenty of fun activities on offer for grandparents and grandchildren so there's no need to feel cut off:

- Go along to coffee mornings with parent and toddler groups.
- You'll love music groups for babies from six months.
- Swimming – once your grandchild is immunized. Ask at a local pool about parent and baby sessions, and they'll welcome grandparents.
- Baby movement classes may be run at leisure centres for babies from six months of age and can be a good opportunity for bonding.
- Baby massage classes, probably run by a natural health centre or local yoga teacher, can help bring you very close to your grandchild.

Many National Trust properties have lots of child-friendly activities and special events as well as wonderful gardens, which you will both enjoy. For information on sites in England, Wales and Northern Ireland, look at www.nationaltrust.org.uk or phone 0870 458 4000. For The National Trust for Scotland, look at www.nts.org.uk or phone 0844 493 2100.

Wherever you go, you should be prepared to make endless stops to look at anything that catches your grandchild's attention. But you have the time. Always take enough drinks and snacks to keep him happy for the full duration of the trip. Don't take on a trip of any kind if you or he are feeling out of sorts; the day is bound to be a disaster, so don't feel guilty about cancelling an outing altogether.

Going shopping Before you leave for a shopping expedition on your own with your grandchild, ask your children for advice on the most baby-friendly stores in their area.

Most supermarkets and department stores provide facilities to help anyone with a baby. Shopping malls can be more difficult if they're on more than one level, but most have lifts as well as escalators.

● When you're in a supermarket, always use a supermarket trolley that's appropriate to your grandchild's size and weight and strap her into the seat with a harness. Be aware that she may try to grab items off the shelves.

● Shopping tends to make children hungry and therefore fretful. Avoid this by taking a snack and drink with you, or let them choose something from the shelves that they can munch on as you go round, and then pay for it at the checkout.

● Use any crèche facilities that are available if you need to do some shopping by yourself.

Baby facilities to look out for

Here are some ideas for facilities to look out for when planning a shopping trip with your grandchild.

Parking spaces
Some stores have dedicated parent and baby parking spaces close to the entrance that grandparents can use too.

Wider checkouts
Good supermarkets have at least two wider-than-average checkouts to accommodate prams.

Special discounts
Some stores offer discounts for parents or grandparents with a baby under 12 months.

Babycare
Supervised crèches are available at some stores as long as you're there to be called if necessary.

Changing and feeding
Many stores have a baby changing area in their toilets, but if you're happy just to sit out of the way to feed your grandchild, ask an assistant.

Shopping with a grandchild

Once your grandchild can walk, losing her in a crowd can be a worry, so take some steps against this happening.

- Use reins or a wrist strap when you're in busy places so she can't wander.
- Dress your toddler grandchild in something brightly coloured so that you can spot her from a distance.
- Have some sort of **family code** as a signal for your grandchildren to come back to you. My father had a special whistle for us, but as I can't whistle I used to carry a small whistle around my neck so I could let my kids know where I was. Now I do the same with my grandchildren.
- All shopping trips can be **lessons**. For instance, you can teach your grandchild about healthy eating – fresh vegetables are better than tinned.
- From as early an age as possible, make sure your grandchild learns her name, address and telephone number, so she can repeat it if she gets lost when she's with you.
- Teach her **never** to walk off with a stranger.
- Make sure your grandchild can recognize her surroundings when she's near to home by pointing out **landmarks** on every journey: "There's the pillar box on the corner, and there's the blue gate and our house is the next one along."

You can use shopping trips as opportunities to teach your grandchild all sorts of things – colours, for example: "This tin is red; that packet is blue; that jar has a yellow wrapper". Any child will recognize the cereal packet that he sees at breakfast every morning and will soon understand what the words mean. From as early as 18 months, you can say to your grandchild, "Can you see the cereal you like? Now I wonder where the jam is?" Early reading can be encouraged by teaching your grandchild to associate the contents of a packet or tin with things that he actually eats at home. For example, if he drinks cocoa regularly, you only have to take the tin of the brand he sees every day from the shelf and ask "What does this word say?" for him to respond with "Cocoa", because he has learned from experience that cocoa is what comes out of that tin. All my children began to read food packets before they read anything else.

When your grandchild is older, trips to the supermarket can also be a chance to learn about the act of shopping itself, and the choosing and decision-making that are involved. You can introduce him to the value of money, and to a certain degree you can teach him about manners and sociability, because he'll very quickly learn the justice of allowing other people to get to the shelves when he has a great interest in doing so himself.

You can use shopping trips as opportunities to teach your grandchild all sorts of things

Keeping your grandchild close to you

Because babies are always grasping and reaching for interesting objects, walk down the centre of the aisle so that she's not tempted to dislodge tins and packets from the shelves. One way to control her is to keep her interested, and you can do this by keeping up a running commentary, with observations or questions that engage her. Your young grandchild will love being involved in shopping decisions, and she'll feel very important and needed if you act on her preferences. With items where brand isn't important to you, ask her to select products by pointing to the one she would like you to buy. As my grandchildren get older and can toddle round with the shopping trolley, I ask them to put all their choices into the shopping trolley themselves, so that they're constantly engaged in looking for their favourite things, feeling a great sense of achievement in filling up the trolley. At the checkout you can take out those things you don't want, without your grandchild seeing.

One of the ways I distract and entertain my grandchildren on a shopping trip is to ask them if they're thirsty or hungry immediately on entering a supermarket, and buy them a drink or a healthy snack. That way they can munch or sip their way around the supermarket and feel quite happy and occupied the whole time. If, however, you have a wayward grandchild who keeps on getting into mischief, the only way to handle the situation may be to keep her on reins or a wrist strap to prevent her from wandering off and getting lost.

*Your young grandchild will love **being involved** in shopping decisions*

Going out in the car

Children can be very active on car journeys. They're learning and taking great pride in newly acquired physical skills, like jumping, skipping, hopping, climbing and running, and it's very difficult for them to be confined in a small space. All this is intensified in hot weather, when young children tend to become tired, touchy and tearful more easily than when the temperature is equable.

Baby on board

In your own car or your children's, it's a good idea to keep the following important items of equipment more or less permanently ready for trips with your grandchildren:

- Car seat correctly fitted and with safety harness
- A blind to block out bright sun
- A bag with basic changing and feeding equipment; remember to check it and restock regularly
- Baby travelling toys
- A rug
- A couple of favourite CDs
- Tissues
- A CD player and favourite CDs will keep your grandchild happy and you can concentrate on the driving
- If you can afford one, a DVD player with DVDs suitable for his age will be a godsend for an older grandchild

Your journey checklist   With any kind of outing with your grandchildren, the essential thing is to plan and prepare well in advance. The following tips will all help to make things go more smoothly for you:

- Try to start travelling early in the morning or at night, when the roads are empty.
- Carry a large bag of spare clothes for your grandchild; be philosophical about accidents, and change him readily into dry clothes if necessary.
- For safety, tape cutlery to the inside of food containers.
- Take some soft clothing like an anorak or sweater that your grandchild can use as a pillow.
- Have a supply of bags into which cartons, bottles and wrappers can be placed after use.
- Take a box of baby wipes to clean sticky hands and faces.

Rear-facing car seats make travelling by car with a young baby relatively trouble-free, but your car seat must be correctly fitted. Never use a rear-facing baby seat in the front in a car with airbags, unless you can switch off the airbag. In a crash an airbag will hit the baby seat and could be fatal for your grandchild. Correct fitting is equally important when your baby grandchild graduates to a front-facing seat in the back.

Most babies are lulled to sleep by the movement of a car, but a hungry baby will wake and become upset. If you're on your own, find a safe place where you can park and feed her; it's better than trying to drive on with a screaming baby, which will make you both tense. Take a few nappies, wipes and nappy sacks in the car for emergencies. Remember the sun can be a problem for babies, so use a detachable blind on your car window to provide shade.

If you're like me you'll always feel like indulging your grandchildren but, in a car, shouting and kicking shouldn't be tolerated; it's extremely distracting for you while you're driving and could even be dangerous. If your grandchild does behave badly on a journey, pull straight over to the side of the road, stop the car, and sort out the difficulty. Simply tell your grandchild that you're going no further until he starts to behave himself.

It's essential to plan and prepare **well in advance** *when going on an outing with grandchildren*

Longer journeys Most children will become restless if they have to travel for more than an hour and a half. Young children have no idea of time, so they'll be constantly asking you when you're going to arrive, or whether you're nearly there. Restlessness can be alleviated by stopping the car every hour for about five minutes and allowing your grandchildren to run around, explore, have a loo-break and a drink, and generally get rid of excess energy.

Your grandchild will get bored and hungry, so always have some nutritious snacks like raisins, sugarless cornflakes, or pieces of cheese in plastic bags, and take more drinks than you ever think you'll need, as her capacity for liquid is greatly increased when she's travelling. Seedless grapes make a very useful snack because they quench her thirst as well as satisfying her hunger.

Toys and games You'll need toys to occupy your grandchild while travelling. Books may be a bad idea, though, if she suffers from motion sickness. Buy or make a special cover for the front headrest of your car with pockets in the back which can carry drinks, snacks and toys, or tie toys to coat hooks or handles so that they don't get lost under seats. Magnetized games are particularly useful in cars because the bits cannot get lost. You can also stick Velcro on certain toys so that they will adhere to the car seat and stay in one place while your grandchild's playing with them.

I always find it best if I ask my grandchild to choose some of the toys that she wants to take, and let her be responsible for putting them into her bag. CDs with music or children's stories or a DVD player and discs may give you at least half an hour of peace, so always have some at the ready. "I spy" games are always a favourite, particularly if you join in, and will keep your grandchild occupied for a quite a long time if you make the objects interesting. Keep a special treat tucked away with which to relieve tension or tears.

Going on holiday

If you're going away with a very young grandchild or you're helping your children on a trip, you may feel more comfortable not going abroad in case you need medical help. Having said this, small babies – especially breastfed ones – often travel abroad very well, but it's sensible to take out adequate medical insurance. Whatever the age of the baby, when you're away you'd be well advised to:

- Check how far you're going to be from a doctor's surgery, medical centre or hospital
- Make sure the cot in your holiday accommodation conforms with

Tips for preventing motion sickness

If you have suffered motion sickness, or there's any history of migraine, eczema or allergies in the family, then your grandchild is quite likely to suffer from motion sickness too. There are some things that you can do to help make him comfortable.

- As a preventive, **don't drive fast** or swing around corners.
- Don't give him a rich or greasy meal before a journey.
- You can give a motion-sickness drug, available from doctors, about half an hour before you leave.
- Car sickness can be brought on by **anxiety** and excitement, and is much more likely to happen on the outward journey, so be patient when you leave home.
- **Snacks** that can be sucked are a good idea, because they don't create a mess; take along a supply of glucose sweets.
- Keeping your grandchild **occupied** helps prevent car sickness, but don't let him read, as this may bring it on.
- If you notice your grandchild becoming pale or quiet ask him if he wants to stop. Get him to close his eyes until you reach a safe place to stop, then get him out of the car and be very sympathetic if he actually is sick. Give him **time to recover** before you continue your journey, with him lying down on the back seat if that's possible and drive sedately.
- A supply of **baby wipes** will help you clean up your grandchild (and the car if necessary) should he be sick.
- Give him a drink to get rid of the taste of vomit.

safety standards – the tour operator, travel agent or tourist information office should be able to reassure you on this. Alternatively, take your own travel cot – modern designs are safe and compact.

● Always make sure your grandchild is well protected from the sun: use adequate sunscreen lotions, dress her in protective clothing and keep her in the shade.

Never think your grandchild is too young to travel. Children nearly always surprise us, and rise to the occasion in ways we don't expect. Travelling with young babies is the norm in my family: I'm told that when I was only six weeks old, my mother and father took me camping, living under canvas for two weeks by the sea! When my third son was only ten weeks old we took him to Italy, and while we were finding our lost luggage in Rome, he was by far the best behaved of all of us. He even philosophically accepted my efforts to find the right formula for him, which took three days.

Never think your grandchild
*is **too young** to travel*

Before you go on holiday alone with your grandchild Taking your grandchildren away on holiday alone or with your partner is an ambitious project. You'll remember the glitches that used to occur when you travelled with your own young family and how to sort them out. But much has changed since then. It's as well to check everything out and plan meticulously.

When my four boys were young, my mother and father used to take them away for a fortnight's holiday each year while they were still able, and I'm hoping to do the same thing with my grandchildren. My plan is to take one grandchild at a time so that each one gets my full attention and we spend lots of time just one-on-one, making the holiday really bonding and special. I think this one-to-one time is especially soothing for a grandchild who's feeling dethroned by the arrival of a new baby. In one fell swoop you can restore their confidence, sense of security and self-belief, and you'll make a friend for life.

A golden rule if you're going abroad on holiday is to make sure that your hotel has facilities for children, and that the staff really like children. Things to look for in a hotel include such child facilities as a crèche, a place where you can take your grandchild for early supper, a children's menu, high chairs and cots, a playroom, and an outdoor play area with trained attendants. It's worth going to some trouble to ensure these things are available, because if your grandchildren aren't happy, you won't enjoy the holiday yourself.

Vaccination   Well ahead of time – six months at least – take advice on what vaccinations or immunizations are needed for you and your grandchildren, because regulations are constantly changing. The reason for starting early is that some vaccinations need quite a long lead time. For others, such as hepatitis, you may have to wait four to six weeks between injections, or you may not be able to follow one vaccination immediately with another. You can get information from your doctor, or from major outlets of your travel agent. Some travel agents have doctors on the premises who can give you vaccinations and vaccination certificates, plus any medication you might need such as water-sterilizing tablets.

What to pack

Use the following checklist to make sure you've got everything you need for your grandchild.

- Passport and inoculation documents
- The baby bag (see page 119)
- Pushchair
- A vacuum flask for cool drinks
- Favourite toys and games, books and CDs
- DVD player and discs
- Sun hat, swimwear and flotation items
- Non-crease, drip-dry, UV-resistant clothes
- Plenty of changes of clothes
- Water resistant sunblock and after-sun cream for sunburn
- Anti-sting cream
- Insect repellent cream
- Children's antihistamine medicine
- Children's paracetamol or ibuprofen

Air travel Most airlines make special facilities available to children as long as they're given warning. Try to book a flight that won't be too crowded. Given that children can be unpredictable, it's essential that you make very careful plans, and if possible don't travel alone – have your partner or another family member with you. If you are alone, find out if the airport offers special porterage services for people travelling alone with young children – some do.

Here are some things to think about before you travel:

- Put all travel documents in a special folder, inside a light-weight shoulder bag.
- Aim to reach the airport early enough to avoid long check-in queues, and give yourself plenty of time to get there.
- Make sure that everything you take on board with you has an indestructible label.
- Take a few of your grandchild's favourite toys with you.
- Take your grandchild to the loo just before getting on the plane.
- Take a folding pushchair to the plane with you: the crew will take it from you as you enter, and return it as you leave.
- Children feel some pain during the take-off and landing, so keep aside a little treat for your grandchild so she can suck on it to equalize the pressure in her ears.
- Take a favourite snack and a drink for the plane.

Taking care in the sun Children can get heatstroke in a very short time, and it's a dangerous condition. Most often it occurs when the nape of the neck is exposed to hot sun. On arrival at a sunny resort never expose your grandchild's skin to direct hot sun for longer than the table indicates (see page 139). Though the times in the sun seem short, please adhere to them and make sure your grandchild wears T-shirts and sun hats the rest of the time. He should wear a sunscreen all the time he's outdoors – even if he's swimming or if the weather is cloudy, as he could still burn.

If there have been no untoward effects after the first six days, you can extend the exposure up to several hours, provided your grandchild's perfectly happy and his skin doesn't become inflamed. Remember, too, that children sweat a lot more than adults do in a hot climate, so always carry some water with you and let your grandchild drink as much as he wants.

Protection from the sun Children don't have very much skin pigment, so they have less protection than adults from the sun's ultraviolet rays. Being exposed to direct sunlight can lead to skin damage and skin cancer later in life. To protect your grandchild:

- Use sunscreen of at least factor 25 in addition to the natural protection of clothes and shade. Twenty minutes before going out, apply the lotion to the face, neck, ears, backs of hands and feet.
- In very hot weather, avoid taking her out in the sun between 11am and 4pm. Be aware that she's still at risk on cloudy days.
- Dress her in a wide-brimmed hat and protective clothing, such as a shirt with sleeves and a collar.
- Make sure the pram or buggy has a protective hood or umbrella to shade her.
- Dress your child in a sun hat and UV-resistant T-shirt and shorts, and apply sunscreen regularly when she's outside playing in the sun.

Grandpa comes into his own! Given a man's extra strength and stamina, grandpa might like to carry your grandchild in a sling or pop him in a backpack on outings. All my grandchildren have loved being carried in grandpa's backpack, from where they can survey the world like a little prince or princess. Remember:

- A backpack is more convenient for an older baby than a buggy if you like to do a lot of walking.
- The baby can see what's going on around him.
- Choose a backpack with a holdall for wipes, tissues, drink, snacks and so on.

Safe sun

There are many types of **sunscreen** available. Use one that protects against both UVA and UVB rays, with a sun protection (SP) factor of at least 25. What the SP factor means is that you can stay in the sunshine that number of times longer without getting burned than you could have without the cream; if your grandchild would normally burn after 10 minutes, then with a sunscreen of SP factor 10 she should be able to stay in the sun for 100 minutes without getting burned.

Many sunscreens say that they're waterproof, but if your grandchild's running in and out of the sea or swimming pool, **reapply** sunscreen every half an hour or so.

Under other conditions reapply sunscreen to your grandchild's skin every two hours or so.

Exposure times

Only allow your grandchild to be exposed to hot sun for a very short time at first, and increase the time gradually.

Day 1	5 minutes
Day 2	10 minutes
Day 3	15–20 minutes
Day 4	20–30 minutes
Day 5	45 minutes
Day 6	60 minutes

6 Staying fit for grandparenting

Staying fit at any age is always well worth the effort, but for grandparents there's the bonus of being able to join your family and grandchildren in almost any activity they suggest. As far as your grandchildren are concerned, age doesn't disbar you from any activity. Physically speaking, their expectations of you are high, and if you have any ambitions to fulfil them you'll need to pursue fitness and suppleness.

A few days ago my two-year-old granddaughter encouraged me to "Cover up under my umbrella, Granny", and expected me to sink nimbly to my knees and bend my neck to be the same height as her. So being fit enough to enjoy and play with your grandchildren is the level of fitness to aim for. This doesn't mean being able to run a half marathon or cycle ten miles, but you do need the strength and stamina to walk and play in the park for the best part of three hours or get on the floor to build a farm or have an imaginary tea party. As your grandchildren get older it may include being nimble enough to scramble up and down a river bank on a fishing expedition or being able to play games in the swimming pool until you're out of breath.

being fit enough to enjoy and play with your grandchildren is the level of fitness to aim for

A get-up-and-go grandparent

Paying attention to what you eat and taking regular exercise are a small price to pay to be a get-up-and-go kind of granny or grandpa. If this sounds like too much effort, think of the benefits: weekends and holidays with the children because you can keep up; following a passionate hobby together; enjoying the outdoors through energetic sports such as skiing and horse riding. And being that kind of grandparent may even protect you from Alzheimer's.

Yes, it takes determination and application, but you're an expert at that and you wouldn't want to stay at home and stiffen up, would you? Plus, you'll never be alone. You'll always have companionship because you're an up-for-it kind of person who will be interesting to your grandchildren.

Why we need exercise

Your grandchildren could be doing you a great favour in giving you the motivation to stay fit. Inactivity causes problems because our metabolism is geared to use the energy we take in as food, and without activity that surplus energy cannot be got rid of. It accumulates in the only way the body knows how, as fat. Think of your toddler grandchild. Toddlers are called toddlers because they "toddle" most of the time. They're never still and they rarely rest. Your toddler grandchild is an example of the human body in an ideal state, not just for two- and three-year-olds, but for as long as we live. Imitate your grandchild by keeping active. No need for jogging at lunchtime or cycling in the afternoon. Walking, gardening, dancing and the "soft" martial arts like tai chi are all ideal. Just keep your body on the move for spells of a few hours each day and you'll stay fit.

So the message is not more strenuous, high-impact exercise. It's much more appealing than that – all you have to do is stay on your feet for as many hours as you can every day. Brisk walking is the nearest you have to get to a workout.

Exercise and mental wellbeing Physical activity can stop you being a moody grandparent because it boosts your mental wellbeing as well as your physical, and changes your outlook on life. I know from

This is what happens when we're inactive

Loss of muscle strength

We lose ten per cent of muscle mass every ten years after 65
but
exercise increases the size and strength of your muscles, including your heart. Stronger arms and legs help keep you mobile and able to carry heavy bags – and lift toddlers.

Loss of bone calcium

Woman lose a third to a half of bone density by the age of 90, increasing the risk of bone fracture. One in four women with a fractured hip will die
but
weight-bearing exercise keeps your bones healthy, improves your balance and lessens the risk of falling and breaking brittle bones.

Loss of heart/lung efficiency (breathlessness)

Most people lose more than half their cardiovascular fitness between the ages of 20 and 80
but
exercise stops this. It prevents heart disease and other chronic diseases and increases your life expectancy.

personal experience that regular physical exercise lifts my mood and helps me deal with negative emotions like anger and depression. Exercise brings a general sense of optimism as well as making you feel in good physical condition.

I've noticed that if I wake up feeling a bit down and out of sorts, 30 minutes on my exercise bike helps me feel better. That's because the exercise floods my body with hormones that reduce tension levels and feelings of stress and fatigue. There's no time-lag. These changes happen right away, even though I don't pedal that strenuously, and the effects can last for eight hours.

Exercise makes you feel better about yourself A grandparent suffering anxiety and low self-esteem isn't much fun, and exercise can help. Studies have shown people soon feel better about themselves once they start an exercise programme. Changes to body shape and stronger muscles improve your self-image, which in turn boosts your mental wellbeing. Exercise helps you to see just what you're capable of and gives you a sense of achievement. Learning a new skill or achieving a goal, however small, boosts self-esteem and motivation. Exercise is an excellent antidepressant: brisk walking or cycling are well known to help people who have moderate to severe depression.

Exercise brings a general **sense** *of optimism as well as making you feel in good physical condition*

Exercise protects you from cancer Living long enough to see your grandchildren grow up is every grandparent's dream, and you can protect your health with exercise. Physically active men and women have half the risk of their sedentary friends of getting colon cancer. The protection may be due to the beneficial effect of exercise on insulin, prostaglandins and bile, all of which cause overgrowth of the colon lining. Exercise also speeds up your bowel movements, cutting down the length of time that faecal carcinogens are in contact with your colonic lining.

The hormones implicated in breast and uterine cancer are modulated by exercise. Studies show that physical activity can be responsible for a *30 per cent reduction in breast cancer rates,* and the more exercise you take, the greater the protection. So exercise probably protects against cancer forming. And it may protect against recurrence and survival after a cancer has been diagnosed. The evidence is strongest for colon and breast cancer, but moderate activity like walking and cycling should be part of everyone's cancer-protection programme.

Exercise keeps your heart elastic With boisterous grandchildren you never know when you're going to call on your heart to perform a superhuman task. If your heart has been allowed to become slack and fat it won't be able to respond in an emergency. Exercise can make your heart fit enough to pull out the stops in more ways than one.

When you exercise, you increase the ability of your heart and lungs to adapt to any sudden increase in the work they have to do. Exercise opens up spare arteries to your heart muscle, ensuring that blood will reach the hard-working tissues, even if one of the arteries gets blocked off. In these two ways, exercise can lower your risk of a heart attack. It also lowers your blood pressure, thereby reducing the risk of stroke.

Key benefits of exercise

- "Growth" hormones make new brain cells grow, so cognitive thinking and memory improve.
- **Endorphins** give you an eight-hour high.
- Exercise regulates your appetite and stops you having cravings and bingeing on food.
- Exercise hormones treat anxiety and depression, so lessening the need for antidepressants.
- Helps irritable bowel syndrome.
- **Lowers** blood pressure.
- Reshapes your body.
- Good for migraine, cures headaches.
- Helps you sleep better.
- Increases heart/lung efficiency so you can be more active.
- **Lowers** cholesterol so you're less likely to have heart attacks or strokes.
- Good for bones, so less osteoporosis.
- Increases suppleness, mobility and stamina.
- Better balance, so fewer falls.

moderate activity
like walking and cycling should
be part of everyone's
cancer-protection programme

Look after your back

The spine is one of the most over-worked areas of the body. It's subjected to constant stress and strain, even when you're in bed if your mattress and pillows aren't back-friendly. Once you have grandchildren, your back may be put under extra stress as you'll want to pick up babies and children, cuddle them and carry them around – even a small child can feel surprisingly heavy after the first few minutes. It's important to maintain good posture when lifting or carrying your grandchildren, or bending. Not only does it make life easier, it also saves unnecessary wear and tear on muscles and joints. Here are some tips to remember.

- **Kneel** right down when doing something at floor level, such as playing with your grandchild or weeding.
- **Avoid stooping,** which is very tiring and a strain on the back: just sit down.
- When lifting a child, or anything heavy such as a pushchair, bend down from your **knees**, not your waist.
- Carry a child or a heavy package **close** to your body, not out in front, and bend when putting the child or package down again.
- To shift a big object, **push with your back**, not your hands. It's always best to ask for help.
- Strong **abdominal muscles** "splint" the back, so pull them in and count to five whenever you remember.

Exercise controls your appetite Staying trim helps to keep you agile, and exercise is key. We all have something called the *appestat*, a switch in the brain that tells us we're full and should stop eating. All day long the appestat is bombarded with messages (chemical, electrical, hormonal, psychological) that turn it on and off. Exercise turns it on (STOP EATING!), and it turns it on for as long as you exercise every day. The effects of this turn-on are both subtle and unsubtle. First of all you don't feel hungry for an hour or so after exercising because exercise flattens your insulin levels, removing your desire to eat.

Because of this stabilization of insulin, the appestat becomes highly sensitive and starts to give you really early signals that you've had enough. That's the time to stop eating. Exercise makes you listen to your appestat. You eat less, lose weight and keep it off.

All you have to do is walk

You're going to have to walk quite long distances with your grandchild so here are a few things to think about when you first take up walking as exercise:

- You're not in a hurry.
- Measure progress not in days but in weeks.
- At the end of four weeks' regular brisk walking I guarantee you'll notice *changes* in your body and your mental wellbeing, and you'll be more than ready to push a pram around the park when your grandchild arrives.
- As you're going to take it easy, don't worry about measuring your heart rate, just get up and go.
- All you have to aim at is to walk for half an hour at a pace slightly above a stroll.

- To start with, walk on level ground and avoid hills.
- Always walk "within your breath". This will mean that your heart is beating at about 60 per cent of its maximum rate.
- Never push yourself further than you feel you want to go, and as soon as you feel strain, stop.
- Don't try to increase the speed at which you walk, but try to increase the distance or the time you spend walking.
- At the beginning, never walk into the wind. This will increase your workload by quite a lot, especially if you have heart problems.
- Work at your walking until you're able to walk about 5 km (3 miles) without stopping in an hour.
- Good walking shoes are key, so make sure your feet are comfortable and wear good walking socks.
- Wear layers that you can peel off if necessary or put on when it gets a bit colder. Make sure they're loose-fitting.
- If you possibly can, keep to your plan of regular exercise. Walk a minimum of three times a week. Once you have grandchildren a regular walk can be a lovely thing to do together and good for both of you.
- A good tip is to walk a useful journey that you might otherwise do by car – for example, to the shops or train station so it becomes a daily pattern.

What if you're not so able

Not all grandparents can achieve the level of fitness they'd like and some, due to disability or illness, can't get out very much. Of course you still want to have fun with your grandchildren, but infirmity means that few outings can be spontaneous and may require pre-planning and the presence of helpers.

Tips for starting to take exercise

You have nine months' warning of a grandchild's arrival so start exercising gently. There's no hurry.

- **Always** check with your doctor before you start exercising.
- Choose activities and exercises that you enjoy or you'll find it hard to stick to your programme.
- Exercises shouldn't be a chore – if they are, you're doing the wrong ones.
- Exercises should never be physically punishing – if they are, you're pushing yourself too hard.
- If you can't carry on a **conversation** while exercising, the activity is too strenuous.
- The best form of exercise is one that **fits in** with your daily life, like taking the dog for a walk, cycling to work or to the shops, or climbing stairs rather than taking the lift.
- **Never** exercise on a full stomach. Always wait at least an hour, and spend a few minutes loosening up before beginning any kind of strenuous exercise.
- **Never** be overzealous about increasing the amount of time you spend exercising. Slowly and surely should be your motto.
- Once you've reached your desired level of fitness try to exercise three or four times a week to maintain it.
- Simply increasing the amount of **walking** you do will increase your fitness.
- The aim isn't to exercise strenuously three times a week, it's to **exercise gently** every day.

But where there's a will there's a way. A girlfriend of mine is confined to a wheelchair due to multiple sclerosis, but nonetheless spends much joyful time with her four grandchildren. Once a week her grandchildren come to her and she makes sure she has a couple of friends in to help. And once a week she spends a day with her daughter and the children. Granted, she's adapted her car for wheelchair travel and she's not short of a helping hand, but her severe disability hasn't curtailed her activities one jot.

And then there's a grandpa I know who has had the lower part of his right leg amputated and has had a "bionic" one fitted. He started playing tennis again because one of his grandsons wanted to knock up with him, and he's continued skiing so that he doesn't miss out on family skiing holidays with his grandchildren each Christmas.

car journeys and train journeys can be **enjoyable** *ends in themselves*

One strategy that less fit grandparents can use to make every outing exciting is to emphasize the means of transport rather than the destination. So car journeys and train journeys can be enjoyable ends in themselves. On a shipboard holiday with your grandchildren you could lounge safely on deck while you watch them excel at water sports, and hearing about their scuba-diving can be almost as exciting as doing it yourself. You may not be able to go up in a hot-air balloon with them, but you can arrange the outing for them, watch from the car and hear vivid descriptions of their adventures when they're back on terra firma. A helicopter ride may be beyond you, but you can get everyone to the airport and hear about the amazing things they saw and learned when they return from the trip. You can probably accompany your grandchildren to any leisure or theme park where there's disabled access, and that includes Disney. Just think of organizing a trip to Paris or Florida!

My recipe for enjoying life for as long as possible

I'm forced to the conclusion that there is no single elixir of life, no pill, no potion, no single food, no single rule. However, there is a LIFESTYLE, which includes most of the above, but it requires more effort than simply reaching for a bunch of supplements.

To live longer you have to invest, work, commit and remain vigilant. Even if my recipe doesn't result in a single extra day of life, I can promise you you'll have more life in every day you live.

- Have porridge oats for breakfast.
- Don't eat fatty foods, except oily fish.
- Eat fruit and vegetables at every meal if possible.
- Eat fresh food whenever you can.
- Eat fish, especially oily fish, whenever you can.

Eat right, stay well and enjoy your grandchildren

Exercise is the key to staying fit and trim, but what you eat can do a lot to change the way you look and feel. Eating healthily can certainly increase your wellbeing and may contribute to your lifespan, giving you the chance of staying active and healthy for as long as you live.

Start by looking at how much of your diet relies on fresh foods. By fresh foods I mean ingredients that you buy fresh and cook yourself, such as vegetables, meat and fish. It's true that certain processed foods like wholemeal bread, tinned oily fish and frozen (not tinned) vegetables can effectively deliver the nutrients they started out with and which we need. However, most processed foods lose nutrients in the processing and they include quantities of ingredients that we should definitely steer clear of: fat, salt and sugar. The healthiest diet for people of any age is based on fresh foods, with at least five portions of fruit and vegetables a day, preferably more.

Learn by heart which foods are high in which vitamins and minerals. For instance:

- Good sources of FOLIC ACID are spinach, curly kale, beet greens, legumes and nuts.
- Good sources of VITAMIN B6 are seafood, whole grains, bananas, nuts and poultry.
- VITAMIN E is concentrated in vegetable food containing fats, such as soya beans, sunflower and corn oils, nuts and seeds, whole grains and wheatgerm.
- You get SELENIUM in grains, sunflower seeds, meat, garlic and seafood – especially tuna, swordfish and oysters – but brazil nuts are the best source of all.
- CHROMIUM is found in brewer's yeast, broccoli, barley, liver, shrimp, whole grains, mushrooms and some beers.

The healthiest diet for people of any age is based on fresh foods, with **at least five portions** *of fruit and vegetables a day, preferably more*

Staying fit

Cut your calorie intake Cutting calories isn't just to control your weight; it's to prolong your life. Calorie restriction extends the life of every animal it's been tried on, sometimes by 50 per cent, so this may also help you be a healthier grandparent. Here are some tips that might help you keep calories down.

● Drink water before you eat. It decreases your appetite, stops you eating too much, helps mix the digestive juices, and makes your stomach produce more acid, which prevents flatulence.

● Eat slowly if you're ravenous. Count to ten before taking a bite and then eat your food slowly. Before swallowing, hold food in your mouth for ten seconds.

● Cut your calories in an instant and satisfy your cravings by chewing sugarless gum or eating a low-calorie menthol mint.

● Put a motto on the fridge door, on your mirror or on your computer to remind you that you don't want to eat high-calorie snacks.

● Chunky soup with large pieces of vegetables makes you feel fuller, and you eat a fifth less than you do of pureed soup.

● Add some chilli to your food. We tend to eat less when food tastes spicy and hot.

Grandparents' golden rules for healthy eating

- Start the day with **porridge** for breakfast.
- Eat at least **five** servings of fruit and vegetables a day, but try for ten. Eat lots of different fruits and vegetables.
- Choose fresh and frozen fruits and vegetables over canned ones where possible.
- Eat both **whole** fruits and vegetables and juices, or blend your own.
- Eat vegetables both **raw** and lightly cooked. Both have advantages.
- To get the most **antioxidants**, choose deeply coloured fruits and vegetables.
- Cook vegetables in a microwave oven to retain as many antioxidants as possible.
- Have nourishing **chunky** vegetable stews when you can.
- **Eat three** or more servings every day of food made with wholegrains. Remember, brown rice contains more nutrients and more fibre than polished rice.
- Make complex, unrefined unprocessed carbohydrates the basis of your diet. More than half of your total calories should come from fruit, vegetables, rice and wholegrains.
- **Limit fat intake** to a third or less of total calories and include health-giving Omega 3 fats found in herrings, sardines, salmon, pilchards, nuts and cod liver oil twice a week at least.

- A lunch box may save you up to 300 calories a day if you make up your own meals.
- Have a cup of tea (black, green or jasmine) before you walk. Fatty acids are liberated from your muscles, so you burn fat faster.
- Add interest to your salads with celery, carrots, broccoli, onions and other vegetables.
- Instead of drinking whole juice, mix half your favourite juice with water and you'll cut up to 100 calories per glass.
- Get into the habit of reading labels for calories per portion.
- Don't pour oil, spray it as the Japanese do for stir-frying. You'll use about six times less than if you pour it.
- Think small portions. Use smaller plates so that your portion of food looks larger.

Antioxidants

As we get older our DNA – the copy-holder of our genes that is present in all of our cells and is copied every time a cell divides or is renewed – begins to get a bit dog-eared. Repeated copying leads to a higher proportion of mistakes, and attacks on DNA by free radicals compounds the damage.

Normal body functions like breathing or digesting food entail chemical reactions that affect the oxygen molecules in our bodies. The chemical reactions rob these molecules of an electron and so result in lots of oxygen molecules that are one electron short. These molecules are known as free radicals. It is thought that damage is caused to cells, and particularly to the DNA within them, by free radicals seeking to replace their missing electron by stealing one from whole molecules. And this process is what's thought to cause ageing. It follows that whatever is capable of rendering free radicals harmless is very good news indeed.

The good news comes in the form of antioxidants. They are the moppers-up of those damaging chemicals known as *free radicals*, which cells turn out every second of the day and night as the result of our metabolism. However, compared to the potent antioxidants our own cells can manufacture, the antioxidants that we might take in a tablet add little.

The emphasis has to be on food, not supplements, as a source of antioxidants. The simple fact is that foods contain thousands of micro-nutrients which help our bodies to use antioxidants and get them to the places they're needed; supplements don't. Eat as much antioxidant-containing food as you can, but popping supplements won't bring you added benefit. The most powerful antioxidants are vitamins C and E, selenium and beta-carotene.

Vitamin C What it does: helps make collagen, the body's natural cement and scaffolding, found all over the body in tendons, cartilage, bones and skin. It aids wound healing, increases iron absorption and protects vitamin E from oxidation. It's important for the health of blood vessels and protects against cataracts, macular degeneration and the irreversible loss of vision found in many old people.
Top sources: blackcurrants, broccoli, Brussels sprouts, cauliflower, strawberries, lemons, cabbage, orange, spinach, grapefruit, pineapple, potatoes, tomatoes, peaches, beans, bananas, peas.

Vitamin E What it does: guards against free radical damage, lowers heart attack and cancer risk, improves immunity, and reduces the risk of dementia. May also help inhibit the development of prostate cancer.

The emphasis has to be on
food, not supplements,
as a source of antioxidants

Top sources: almonds, rapeseed oil, hazelnuts, margarine, olive oil, peanut butter, rice bran, sunflower oil, shrimp, sweet potato, sunflower seeds, wheatgerm oil, whole grains, cereals.

Selenium What it does: essential for a healthy immune system to help us combat infections and cancer. Selenium is also a potent anti-cancer agent and may be particularly important in preventing lung cancer. It protects against heart disease and also seems to have a positive effect on mood and mental functioning by increasing blood flow to the brain.

Top sources: wholegrains, sunflower seeds, meat, seafood (tuna, swordfish, oysters), garlic, brazil nuts.

Beta-carotene What it does: it is thought to help prevent and reverse cancer, heart disease, cataracts and compromised immunity. Beta-carotene also seems to block cancer, particularly cancer of the cervix and the spreading of cancer cells. It may play a part in stopping heart attacks by preventing arteries from clogging with fat; it may even protect against strokes.

Top sources: carrots, sweet potato, apricots, chicory, spinach, cantaloupe, pumpkin, squash, tomato juice, grapefruit, mangoes.

Fruit and veg for active grandparents

- **Broccoli** contains lots of calcium but also a great selection of antioxidants, particularly one called sulphorane, as well as vitamin C, beta-carotene, quercetin, glutathione and lutein. It's also one of the richest food sources of the trace metal chromium, which attacks insulin resistance and helps normalize blood sugar. Broccoli-eaters also suffer less colon and lung cancer and heart disease.

- **Carrots** are a must every day, and legendary in fighting off the effects of ageing. Eat five carrots a week and you'll reduce your risk of a stroke by almost two-thirds. A couple of carrots a day will lower your blood cholesterol by 10 per cent and cut your lung cancer risk by half, even in smokers.

- **Grapes** Red are best. Grapes contain 20 known antioxidants, mainly in the skin and seeds – the more colourful the skin, the greater the antioxidant effect. Grape antioxidants lower LDL cholesterol and relax blood vessels. Three glasses of purple grape juice and one glass of red wine have equal anti-clotting effects in the arteries. Raisins are even more potent than fresh grapes.

- **Berries** The darker the berry, the more antioxidants it has, so go for blueberries, which have an antioxidant called anthocyanon. Both blueberries and cranberries help ward off urinary tract infections. Strawberries may ward off cancer, and all berries are rich in the antioxidant vitamin C.

- **Citrus fruits** The orange contains a vast array of antioxidants, including carotenoids, terpenes, flavonoids and vitamin C. Grapefruit has a unique type of fibre, especially in the membranes and the juice sacs, that reduces cholesterol and may even reverse atherosclerosis.

● **Tomatoes** Never go a day without them. They're practically the only reliable source of the antioxidant lycopene, which preserves mental and physical functioning as we age and lowers the risk of pancreatic and cervical cancer. Cooking and canning tomatoes doesn't destroy lycopene. Cooked tomatoes may even be more cancer-protective than fresh, and may lower the risk of prostate cancer.

● **Cabbage** Like broccoli, cabbage is high in antioxidant activity, and cabbage eaters have a lower risk of colon, stomach and breast cancer. Savoy cabbage is the most potent.

● **Onions** Red and yellow onions are richest in quercetin. Quercetin helps keep bad LDL cholesterol from attacking the arteries and helps prevent blood clots.

● **Avocado** One of the most potent antioxidants. Though avocados contain lots of fat, it's healthy fat in that it lowers blood cholesterol; it also delivers potassium to protect blood vessels.

● **Spinach** may protect against cancer, heart disease, high blood pressure, strokes, cataracts and even psychiatric problems because of its powerful antioxidant lutein. Eating large amounts of spinach may cut the risk of the vision-destroying disease macular degeneration.

7 Planning for the future

All parents and grandparents have dreams and aspirations for their children and grandchildren. To help realize your dreams, some sort of financial planning is nearly always required, and yet finances are often one of the last items on your priority list.

First of all, let me stress that the suggestions that follow are for general information only. When making decisions about your family's finances, always obtain independent professional advice appropriate to your own particular situation.

The importance of financial planning

As your family expands, it rapidly becomes obvious that careful financial planning is necessary if the costs of family life are not going to send your children's bank balances and anxiety levels spiralling out of control. You've brought up children of your own so you know that it's expensive to raise a family. Although some people find money matters confusing or off-putting, a little sound financial thinking, amid the joys of discovering you're about to be grandparents, will pay dividends in the months and years to come.

You may want to help from the start, because the financial cost of having a baby has been estimated to range from 15 to 25 per cent of a family's total income. That sounds like a lot of money, but if you think not only about all the equipment your children will need now – the prams, pushchairs, clothes and car seats – but also about the lifestyle changes that may be necessary over time, then that figure starts to sound quite reasonable.

*a little sound financial thinking will **pay dividends** in the months and years to come*

Think ahead Indeed, think further ahead and the costs of your children becoming parents really start to mount up. When mum's maternity leave is over, your children may have to factor in childcare costs. These can make such a significant dent in the family's income that it might not be worth her going back to work. As the family grows, your children may need to move to a bigger house or want a bigger family car (or one with four doors instead of two). Even further down the track there might be education costs and university costs to consider.

Few grandparents look at their little bundle of joy and immediately start planning his or her financial future and calculating the impact on their children's income. But the reality of family life is that for many parents, keeping finances under control is a constant juggling act, interspersed with financial crises.

The good news is that many of the most burdensome costs of grandchildren are some way into the future – school and/or university fees, weddings and start-up funds. But there are also mounting day-to-day costs as your grandchildren eat, wear and want more. You may have children who are proudly independent and refuse all offers of financial help, but you may find, through no fault of their own, that they need the odd helping hand. Accepting money for their family may make some people feel they have failed as parents, so the subject needs to be broached gently and diplomatically. If on the other hand a child asks for financial help, there's no need for such delicacy, and you'll be their favourite person if you can afford to give a loan to keep them solvent.

Saving for a purpose You might decide that you'd like to make a financial contribution to a specific area of your grandchild's life, like school or university fees. So, for instance, it's been estimated that you

Miriam's mailbag

Q My son-in-law resents me

My son-in-law resents me because I'm the manager of a large supermarket and earn decent money – money I spend on all my grandchildren, including his two. My wife and I have taken them on holiday abroad and for weekends to Disneyland Paris and other places, and he's accusoed me of trying to buy their love. My wife says he's upset because he's unemployed and I shouldn't take his animosity personally. I want to do right by my grandchildren, but his constant surliness is taking the shine off our fun times together.

What's the best way to handle him?

a Back off the big spending for a while

Your son-in-law may feel there's something of a power struggle going on between you two for his children's respect, and he's losing. You're a generous man who gets pleasure from seeing your grandchildren's happy faces, but his unemployed status is making him insecure. Right now you've got it all: a good job and the money to be their fairy grandfather. Perhaps you should back off with the big spending for a while and find activities for you and the children to enjoy that don't require a fat chequebook? This should take the heat off him and the competitive spirit out of your relationship, but you can still enjoy fun times with your grandchildren.

need to start putting away about £200 per month per child from the age of five in order to save enough to pay for the university fees and living expenses of around £9000 a year.

You also need to remember to protect yourself. Apart from the obvious emotional trauma, your death or incapacity could seriously dent your grandchild's financial world. Check you have adequate life and health insurance, plus critical illness cover. Now isn't the time to bury your head in the sand if you want to be in a position to offer financial help. Better to start saving as soon as possible. Saving for children and grand-children is a good way to maximize tax effectiveness while providing for their needs. Policies should normally be written in trust for your children and grandchildren to qualify for maximum tax effectiveness, and getting the right plan for your family's situation is critical.

Last but not least Probably the most constructive thing you can do to ensure your grandchildren have a secure financial future is to teach them how to handle money. Their money management skills develop from the attitudes and spending habits they learn at home, at school and when they're with you. As a grandparent you are ideally placed to teach good money management skills early on, helping your grandchildren become adults who can make sound financial decisions, avoid excessive debt and achieve their own financial goals.

As a grandparent you are ideally placed to teach good money management *skills early on*

Independent advisers can help you shop around the whole market to choose the best company for you as well as the right product. If they give advice on certain types of investments – such as pensions, life insurance, unit trusts, mortgages and shares – financial advisers and the companies they work for must be authorised by the Financial Services Authority, and they must abide by rules designed to protect their customers.

Financial advisers just advising on loans, non-investment ("general") insurance, term insurance or bank and building society accounts don't have to be authorized and are covered by separate rules. To find out whether an adviser or the company they represent is authorized, or should be, ring the Financial Services Authority Consumer Helpline on 0300 500 5000 or go to www.moneymadeclear.fsa.gov.uk/home.

Ways to save for your children and grandchildren

Aside from putting the money straight into a not-to-be-touched high-interest savings account, which is the first essential step (your bank should be able to move any amount saved automatically if you ask them), you can start to be quite creative. And if you're strict about ring-fencing the money, your children and grandchildren will have lots of rainy days to look forward to! You can't save on behalf of your grandchild, but you can save the money yourself and then pay it over to the grandchild, although there might be an inheritance tax liability if you die within seven years.

ISAs ISAs (Individual Savings Accounts) allow you to earn interest tax-free over a year. Over 50s can pay in as much or as little as you like up to £10,200 and you can access the money when you want.

Tips on paying for education

You may want or need to finance a grandchild through private or further education and/or university.

- **Don't** underestimate the amount you'll need. Fees for private schools range from around £7200 to £18,500 a year. University students get by on around £8000–£9000 a year.
- **Do** plan ahead if you can by saving in advance.
- **Do** choose savings schemes that let you withdraw money, as the education costs have to be paid.
- **Do** consider flexible schemes rather than ones that tie you to a particular school or college, unless you're sure your children won't change their minds.
- **Do** check whether your grandchild is eligible for any bursaries or scholarships. You have the time to do this, your children may not have. Contact the school or college and your Local Education Authority (LEA). Some charities may also offer help.
- **Do** check your budget before committing yourself to paying out of your current income.

Check your budget
before committing yourself

There are two types of ISA:

- Cash ISA - maximum investment £5100 cash.
- Stocks and Shares ISA - you can invest the remaining £5100 of your allowance in stocks and shares and insurance if you like.

You can't hold an ISA on behalf of anyone else. You can transfer money saved in a cash ISA to a stocks and shares ISA – but you can't transfer money the other way (www.moneymadeclear.fsa.gov.uk).

Premium bonds Introduced in 1957 as a risk-free lottery, premium bonds are still going strong. Bonds cost £1 each and are entered in a monthly draw for tax-free cash prizes: the most common prizes are £50 and £100, but the jackpot's a million! The maximum amount of premium bonds you can buy is £30,000. There's no interest payable but you can withdraw the whole sum of money at any time without any penalty. Visit the National Savings website at www.nsandi.co.uk for more information.

Giving money to your children and grandchildren

You might want to give money to your children or grandchildren to encourage them to save or as a nest-egg for when they leave home. There's no limit on how much you can give to grandchildren, but if you give money to your children it might be taxed as your income.

However, you can give capital that generates up to £100 of interest to your children without it being taxed – note, each parent has a separate £100 limit. So if both parents contribute equally, your children could get interest of £200 a year each without either of them having to pay tax on it. There's a separate £100 limit for each step-parent too.

Gifts made by grandparents The above £100 limit only applies to parents and step-parents. You can give as much as you like to your grandchildren or other people's children – the interest won't be taxed as your income. However, the children may be liable to pay inheritance tax on the amount they receive, and to pay tax on interest from the income of their savings.

Trust planning The first thing to say is be careful. The rules on this change almost every time there's a budget.

Trust planning can be useful for grandparents who wish to make provision for their grandchildren's education and achieve inheritance tax benefits at the same time. Trusts offer the benefit of transferring the tax liability on future income and capital gains to the children to utilize their personal annual allowances. Chargeable gains on life policies may also be re-assigned, which could avoid a higher-rate tax charge. It's important to take advice on the correct trust arrangements for the investments held.

It's also possible in some circumstances to transfer an existing capital gain to the trust, avoiding the need to settle the tax bill on transfer. The capital gain will later be assessed against the beneficiaries or the trustees; however, indexation relief will be lost. Advice to parents will need to take account of the *parental settlement rules* governing the taxation of gifts to children.

Two types of trust There are basically two types of trust – one in which the children have a right to any income arising from the trust and also own the capital; the other where the distribution of capital and income is at the discretion of the trustees. Accumulation and Maintenance Trusts offer both the above.

Miriam's mailbag

Q What's the best way to save for our grandchild?

Our daughter will soon present us with our first grandchild and we're very excited about it. We'd like to set up a savings account for our grandchild, spread over the long term – say 15–21 years. What would you advise? If possible we'd like something straightforward and simple.

a Here are some options

You have several options open to you. I'm not sure that most financial advisers would recommend a savings account as the most rewarding for you and your grandchild. You'll probably get a better return on the stock market as you have a long time in which to ride its fluctuations and let your money stay put. But basically, there are two possibilities that suit your needs – a maximum investment plan or a unit trust.

• A maximum investment plan is very like an endowment. Your money will be invested in the stock market in the form of either a with-profits investment or a managed fund. You'll have to pay fees of about 5 per cent, but your investment can potentially earn a very good return. On the downside, it's relatively inflexible.

• Your other choice is a unit trust. A useful way of thinking about a unit trust is that it's like a basket into which you can put whatever products you like. It has several advantages: it's more tax-efficient, you have the freedom to make partial withdrawals and you can add money on a regular basis as you can afford it.

• While a simple savings account isn't the best place to leave money for up to 21 years, if, as grandparents, you don't have so much time, you can open a savings account in your grandchild's name. Assuming she isn't a taxpayer, she can earn tax-free interest. Parents can't do this, as a child's income is classified as their own for tax purposes.

• The other option is to open a stakeholder pension for your grandchild. This has the potential to be a lucrative investment, but it's not possible to access stakeholder pensions until the recipient is 55. This is potentially a very tax-efficient way of saving, as for a £2808 investment, £3600 is invested.

• Grandparents can also add to their grandchild's Child Trust Fund account (see page 183).

As grandparents you can open a *savings account* in your grandchild's name

Parental settlement rules assess the income arising from trust assets as the parent's income, which makes it more difficult to benefit from trust planning. However, there's the opportunity to gain immediate benefit through making payment directly to the grandchild's school. "Composite fees" qualify as a disposition for the benefit of a family member, and as such the capital is immediately removed from the estate with a potential IHT saving. There are, though, drawbacks in terms of future potential growth, and you should seek advice in this area before making any decisions.

Trust planning isn't suitable in every situation. If you would like advice in this area contact an experienced adviser.

Children's bank accounts There are plenty of child-specific savings products on offer from banks and building societies eager to attract young customers. Building society accounts are available for children, with interest payable tax-free up to the annual personal allowance (currently £6036).

Normally, when a parent or grandparent invests on behalf of their child, they have to pay tax on the interest if they gift more than £100 a year. But with National Savings Children's Bonus Bonds that doesn't apply. These bonds allow you to set aside for each child a maximum of £3000 in each bond issue. The bonds earn a fixed rate of interest for five years, and after that a bonus is added. At the end of five years, the bonds can be reinvested for another five years, and so on until your child reaches 21 years old. The interest is tax-free. See www.nsandi.co.uk for more information.

Children's bonds from friendly societies (maximum investment £25 a month or £270 a year) normally last for 10 years, but are more open to stock-market fluctuations.

Miriam's mailbag

Q My son is in debt. What's the best way to help his family?

We're grandparents and there's a financial crisis in the family. Our son's family is deep in debt and we're being called upon to dig into our own pockets. We want to help, but what's the best way to do it?

a Help them pay off those debts

Helping your son's family to get out of debt is the single best thing you can do to help their financial position immediately. Getting them into the black may be difficult and they have to work hard, but if you wash your hands of their problem it won't go away and is likely to get much worse. If your grandchild is newly expected, then you could aim to get your family out of debt over the next nine months. If your grandchild's already arrived, you'd be really helping your family if you started helping to pay off those debts today!

If you'd like to do this, there are certain sensible strategies that'll help. First, don't, if possible, let your family take out any more credit – it'll only make their debt bigger. Second, encourage them to get all their paperwork together regarding their current credit cards, who they owe money to, and all their bills and repayment plans. Help them to make a list of all their income and outgoings over a typical week or month. Prioritise those bills that really need to be paid – all the ones

❯

where the creditor can cut off supply (electricity, gas) or threaten court action (mortgage, council tax). For now, ignore the credit card bills – we'll come to those. Just concentrate on the essential ones. Many utility companies offer payment plans allowing bill payments to be staggered over a year instead of having to pay them all at once. Contact each in turn and ask them for more details of payment plans.

It's a good idea to check out rights to alternative sources of income such as child benefits (ask your local Citizens' Advice Bureau for advice on what entitlements there may be, and see below regarding child benefit and tax credits) and check that your family hasn't paid too much tax (contact the Inland Revenue office if you think they're owed a rebate).

Having paid off all the essential weekly or monthly bills they should now know how much they've got left over to make a start on paying off the rest of the credit. Ideally they should pay off their credit card bills IN FULL at the end of each month, so they don't get stung with a huge interest payment on top. However, many people's credit debt is too big for them to manage this. The best way to move forward is to consolidate all credit card bills, transferring all the outstanding balances on to one single credit card – it'll help them know where they stand and they might make a small saving on the interest rate if they shop around for a good deal. Then, work out a staged repayment plan – and stick to

*It's a good idea to check out your rights to **alternative** **sources** of income such as child benefits*

it. If they don't have enough money to pay their bills, contact the Citizens' Advice Bureau for advice on what to do next.

While you're trying to reduce their debt, suggest they alter their buying habits. A dose of retail therapy can be very tempting, but they don't always have to buy new things for their baby. Friends or other family members may be prepared to lend clothes and equipment that their little ones have outgrown, so ask around. There are two important exceptions to this: they should never buy a second-hand car seat, and they should always buy a new cot mattress if they have a second-hand cot.

Of all types of credit card, store cards are particularly dangerous for the unwary. They're usually promoted via attractive-sounding special deals offering large discounts off the first purchase, but their interest rates can be swingeing. It's best to avoid store cards altogether.

Miriam's mailbag

Q **My daughter is a spendthrift. What should we do?**
We just don't know what to do about my daughter's spendthrift lifestyle. She just can't manage the family expenses on a day-to-day basis. We're scared our grandchildren are going to suffer. What's the best way to help?

a **Help her learn how to budget**
With diplomacy and firmness you can guide your family's day-to-day budget management. With household finances, sorting out any credit problems is half the battle won, but many households still run in permanent overdraft. Your child's family may be one of them. And aside from a lottery win or similar unlikely windfall, there's seemingly no escape. However, a little careful budget management can go a considerable way towards lifting your family out of the red. I know that "budget" is a word that makes most people switch off in a second, but I'll try to make this as easy to follow as possible. It's really a question of adopting good habits.

careful **budget management** *can go a considerable way towards lifting your family out of the red*

First, sit down together and make a list of all outgoings (food, bills, fuel, travel costs, clothes etc) over a typical week (or over a month) and then divide it by four to give a rough weekly figure. It might surprise your family just how much money flows through their fingers week by week! Make another list of income and, if they're just squeaking by without managing to save anything, there are plenty of tricks to help them inch their way back from the edge of their overdraft. For instance:

• Encourage paying bills by direct debit. It's often cheaper than paying by cheque, because the payment is cheaper to process, and it'll ensure they won't forget when their payment is due, thus avoiding any costly arrears. You can talk to utility companies about spreading payments – their customer service numbers are on the back of their bills.

• If they're getting stung by large phone bills, Internet bills or utility bills, shop around for a better deal. Since the phone industry was deregulated several years ago, there are many companies vying for business, and many of them offer good deals on weekend calls, cheap rate calls and international calls. It's a cinch to change over to them, too; the family won't need to get a new phone. The same goes for the utility companies – if they switch their provider, then aside from their bills decreasing the only other change should be the logo on the bill itself!

• The same rule – shop around – applies to bank accounts. Banks often try to entice new customers with high interest rates, cashback offers and discounts on purchases, but a few months later the interest rates may have dropped. So why be loyal? As with credit cards, check the financial pages of the papers, find the accounts that are offering the best deals today, and switch!

• Mobile phone bills can be another shocker, but if you encourage your family to use a pay-as-you-go scheme and they are ruthless about restricting mobile use to emergencies or to making travel arrangements on the hoof, the cost will effectively vanish. If they have to use a mobile phone a lot for work, their employer could be asked to buy a phone and to pay the bills too – it's only fair.

• It's wise to cut down on buying highly processed or excessively packaged foods – you're really only paying for the packaging and processing, not the food itself. It may take a bit longer for your daughter and her family to prepare their own food, but it's much cheaper and much, much healthier for them than eating processed foods.

• If possible, cut down on car use – walk or take the bus!

• It isn't always necessary to buy new things. Second-hand is OK! Many items, especially children's clothes and toys, can be picked up for a fraction of their new price at local community second-hand sales, fairs and charity shops. Check the local paper or library for details of sales in their local area.

• Don't over-economise, though. Be alert to bargains but exhort them to buy the best they can afford. If that happens to be the cheapest, then they're in luck! But many very cheap items are actually false economies, lasting for less time and being more costly in the long run than better-quality items.

Government help

There are several types of government help for families, including child benefit, child tax credit and the Child Trust Fund.

Child benefit Child benefit is available to anyone, including grand-parents, bringing up a child under the age of 16. At the time of writing, child benefit amounts to £20 per week for the eldest child who qualifies, and £13.20 per week for each other child who qualifies. This is increased annually. For details, go to www.direct.gov.uk/parents.

Child tax credit As of April 2003 the government launched a new child tax credit, paid directly to the person mainly responsible for looking after the children in a household. Tax credits are available if your income (or you and your partner's joint income) is less than £50,000 a year. Families with lower incomes benefit proportionally more under the scheme.

Child Trust Fund To encourage families to save money specifically for their children, the government has launched a Child Trust Fund scheme, also known as Baby Bonds. Under the scheme, children are eligible for a one-off payment of between £250 and £500, depending on their parents' income. Better still, parents, friends and family will be allowed to contribute up to £1200 per year tax-free.

That's a great leg-up in savings terms, especially for families on lower incomes. You can find out more from www.childtrustfund.gov.uk and from www.thechildrensmutual.co.uk. The Children's Mutual is the government's chosen administrator of these funds and a specialist in children's savings. The scheme began in April 2005 and has been backdated to include babies born on or after September 1, 2002.

Sources of information and advice

Government departments: The Department for Work and Pensions has free leaflets on pensions and information on what your own state pension will be; Inland Revenue for free leaflets on the tax aspects of saving and investing.

The Financial Services Authority: Produces free, user-friendly booklets and fact sheets and can help with general enquiries and complaints-handling procedures.

Newspapers and magazines: Regular articles on savings and investment, and lists of building society and bank interest rates in the personal finance pages of specialist magazines. But check the information given is up to date and accurate.

Libraries: Most libraries have a range of books and magazines on financial services, including Consumers' Association publications and government leaflets. They can also give you details of local advice agencies and help you get information from the Internet.

Trade associations: These often provide free information to help people understand different types of investment and saving.

Individual firms: Most banks, building societies and pension and life insurance companies produce free leaflets. But remember: they want you to buy their products.

Depending on the type of financial product concerned, either the law or non-statutory codes of practice may give you certain rights and protection when you use an adviser.

Useful contacts

Financial Services Authority Consumer Helpline: Tel: 0300 500 5000.
Website: www.moneymadeclear.fsa.gov.uk/register

IFA Promotion: To help you find contact details of financial advisers in
your area. Tel: 020 7833 3131. Website: www.unbiased.co.uk

Institute of Financial Planning: National register of fee-based financial
planners. Tel: 0117 945 2470. Website: www.financialplanning.org.uk

National Savings and Investments: Tel: 0845 964 5000.
Website: www.nsandi.com

Consumers' Association: Now known as **Which?**, the Association
campaigns on issues related to consumer goods, products and services,
including investments. Great source of information about all aspects of
money management. Tel: 01922 822800. Website: www.which.net

The Citizens' Advice Bureau offers a huge range of advice on all types
of consumer investment and other issues. Visit www.nacab.org.uk for
details of your nearest bureau.

The Consumer Credit Counselling Service offers free advice to people
affected by debt. Tel: 0800 138 1111. Website: www.cccs.co.uk

My grandchildren

Name

Birthday

First words

Special names for granny/grandpa

Favourite toys

Name

Birthday

First words

Special names for granny/grandpa

Favourite toys

Name

Birthday

First words

---

*Special names for
granny/grandpa*

Favourite toys

Name

Birthday

First words

---

*Special names for
granny/grandpa*

Favourite toys

My grandchildren

Name

Birthday

First words

Special names for
granny/grandpa

Favourite toys

Name

Birthday

First words

Special names for
granny/grandpa

Favourite toys

Name

Birthday

First words

Special names for granny/grandpa

Favourite toys

Name

Birthday

First words

Special names for granny/grandpa

Favourite toys

Index

Index

Acknowledgements

I'd like to thank my assistant Beth Milner for typing and retyping the manuscript. Thanks also to the *Daily Mirror* readers and to Shelley-Anne Meekcomes and Linda Husband who helped with the interesting scenarios which appear throughout the book.

I'm indebted to my long-term editor and friend Jinny Johnson, who invariably improves my work, and to Kathy Gammon and Marianne Markham, whose willingness to depart from my usual house-style made possible the charming design that's true to the spirit of this book.

My grandchildren Eden, Violet and Brodie inadvertently helped to illustrate the book with drawings they'd given me. A big thank you to them and to Ruby and Alice Martin and Georgina Robinson, whose drawings also appear, and to Euan Grimshaw, whose handwriting appears on the front cover.

The Finnish study mentioned on page 17 is titled 'Fitness benefits of prolonged post-reproductive lifespan in women' and was published in *Nature* 2004 March 11.